Ernesto Saqui
Maya Leader

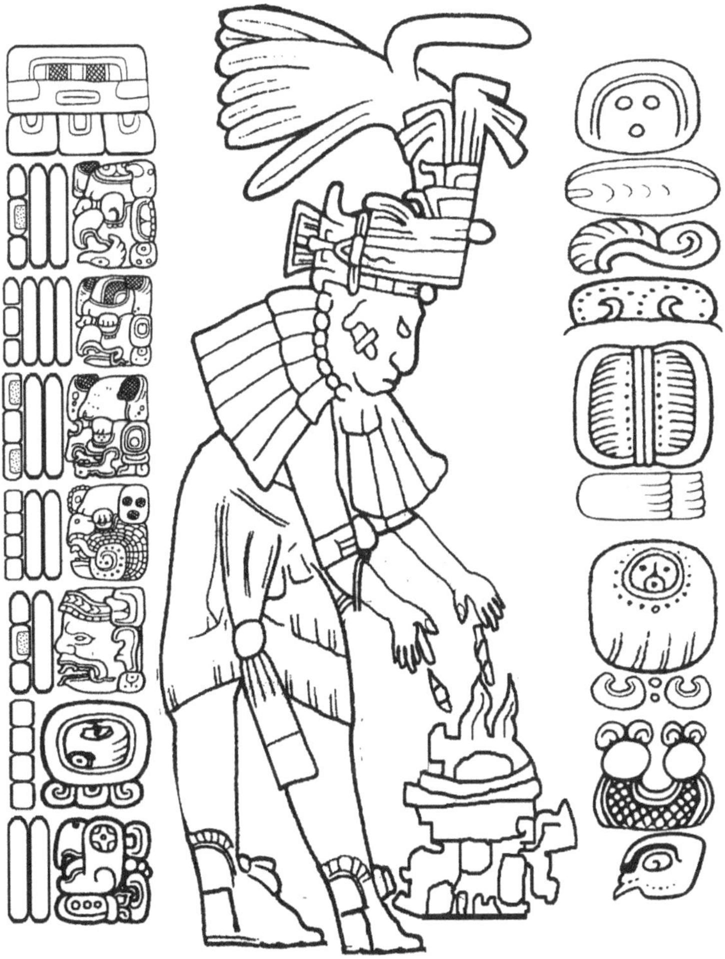

Cover Explanation

The front cover is designed like a Mayan stela as an interpretation of the title of this book with the colours chosen to represent the Mayan cosmology. The background is green which is the centre colour in the Mayan cosmology, representing Mother Earth, the richness, the vegetation, the environment. We are so fortunate to have it. It is our responsibility to care for it, to make or break it, and lately there has been a lot of hurt.

Yellow is the colour of the south. In the Mayan creation story, civilization came from the south. Yellow reminds us of food, of yellow corn. Purple is the colour of the west, of the setting sun. It reminds us that we have come to the end of another day. We have to rest and think about what is next, the unknown. At night you do not see anything. In life we have challenges, barricades we need to pass in terms of health challenges and even death. This is a reminder that we have to keep burning our incense so we can figure out what is next.

The figure in the centre represents Ernesto Saqui performing a ceremony. From recent work by linguists on the Mayan glyphs, it is now possible to use glyph images phonetically to create words. Glyphs were compared with the words they represent in Maya languages and it was determined that certain glyphs consistently represented certain sounds. A list of those is available (Kettunen and Helmke, 2014).

The glyphs on the right side represent the title itself:

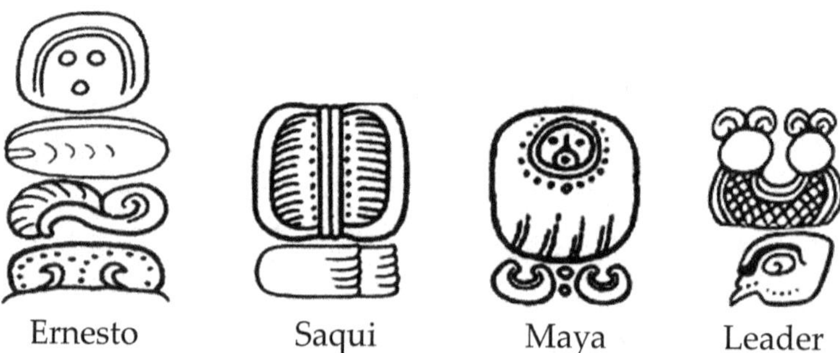

| Ernesto | Saqui | Maya | Leader |

While trying to translate "leader" using the phonetic glyphs available, the sounds we needed for translation of the English — le, li, der — were not available. When we used the word for "leader" in Mopan Maya, "Ch'abe", the glyphs for these sounds were available.

The left side glyphs represent the Mayan calendar date for when Ernesto Saqui was first elected Maya Centre Village Council Chairman, March 5, 1985. The Smithsonian National Museum of the American Indian has provided a website that converts dates in the Gregorian calendar used today into the same date in the Mayan calendar. March 5, 1985, corresponds to the long count (or period) date of 12.18.11.14.7 with 4 Manik' in the Tzolk'in (month) calendar and 10 K'ayab in the Haab (sacred day) calendar.

Every calendar on a stela has some version of what has been called the "calendar glyph" which seems to indicate that a calendar follows. The numbers are on the left side of each glyph. The bars represent five each and the smaller circles each represent one. The circle with an area filled with dots that is in the center of the left column is the Mayan zero, so this is 12, five plus five plus two. The designs of glyphs avoid empty spaces, so zeros are used to fill spaces. All of these calendar glyphs use this same number designations.

Calendar Glyph · 12 baktun

18 katun · 11 tun

14 uinal · 7 k'in

The last two glyphs use Tzolk'in (month) and Haab (sacred day) Mayan calendars.

4 Manik'   10 K'ayab

The Tzolk'in calendar uses sacred names of Gods for the days. This calendar has a cycle of 20 day names and 13 numbers. The 20 day names are in a particular order and change day by day with the next day name and the next number. After 13, the next number begins with one again. At the end of the 20 day names, the next day has the first day name with the next number, cycling through the days. For example, the day before 4 Manik' is 3 Cimi and the day after is 5 Oc.

The Haab Calendar is more like the Gregorian calendar with 18 month names and 20 days in each month. So the day before 10 K'ayab is 9 K'ayab and the day after is 11 K'ayab. After 20 K'ayab, the next day is 1 Cumku and the following day is 2 Cumku, until 20 Cumku and on to the next month name, 1 Pop.

References

Harri Kettunen and Christophe Helmke, 2014. *Introduction to the Maya Hieroglphs.* XIX European Maya Conference, Bratislava. Comenius University in Bratislava, The Slovak Archaeological and Historical Institute.

Michael Coe, 1992. *Breaking the Mayan Code.* New York: Thames and Hudson

Smithonian National National Museum of the American Indian. Living Maya Time Maya Calendar Converter <maya.nmai.si.edu/calendar/maya-calendar-converter>.

Ernesto Saqui
Maya Leader

Ernesto Saqui

Aurora Garcia Saqui, Judy Lumb,
and Dorothy Beveridge, Editors

Producciones de la Hamaca, 2021

Published by *Producciones de la Hamaca* <producciones-hamaca.com>
Caye Caulker, BELIZE
ISBN: 978-976-8273-13-0   (print edition)
ISBN: 978-976-8273-16-1   (e-book edition)

Producciones de la Hamaca is dedicated to:

—Celebration and documentation of Earth
 and all her inhabitants,
—Restoration and conservation of Earth's
 natural resources,
—Creative expression of the sacredness of
 Earth and Spirit.

Table of Contents

Foreword I
Ernesto Saqui: Educator and Leader

I knew Ernesto Saqui as a high school student attending Ecumenical College with the sponsorship of Father Howard Oliver. After he showed leadership as a young boy taking care of the Catholic Church there, Father Oliver thought there was an opportunity to train Ernesto and he would succeed his father in taking care of the church and the village. What he said was prophetic because after graduation Ernesto became the first teacher of St. Jude Primary School in Maya Centre.

Under the guidance of Father Oliver and through my coaching as the Education Officer we were able to give him the capacity to meet that challenge and establish a solid foundation for Maya Centre Primary School with the full support of the Parent Teachers Association and the Village Council with his uncle Eulogio Sho as Chairman. The school started as a one-teacher school, he being the sole Principal and Assistant in charge of all eight grades, from Infant One to Standard Six. He took up the challenge and used his initiative to gather ideas from rubbing shoulders with other teachers at workshops and meetings. I fought for an Assistant and, with the two of them, they managed well. As the school grew, his brother Liberato joined them in the effort to provide primary school education for the children of Maya Centre.

Ambitious Ernesto Saqui did not stop there. He took an interest in a workshop to develop the management plan for Cockscomb Basin Wildlife Sanctuary. He was given two weeks off to attend the workshop and I represented the Department of Education there. What impressed me most was his dedication and commitment to the workshop. I said, "you would be the best person to be the first Park Director of the Cockscomb Basin Wildlife Sanctuary."

Later when he ran for Standard Bearer for the People's United Party, I was his Campaign Manager. There were five or six of us in the group, we would meet at his house, or at my office in Dangriga. We strategized. I told him in politics to make inroads you need to be visible and present. Visit the communities, talk with people, talk with the old heads, the teachers, sell yourself. That is the best way of becoming present in the community. He agreed with that, believed in it, and started visiting the communities and making himself visible.

We kept planning, but we felt that Henry Canton was not comfortable with Ernesto. I think in hindsight Canton was afraid that Ernesto would win. That's why he brought in Elizabeth Zabaneh. If she had not been brought in, Ernesto would have won the Standard Bearer and the election. He had support from the Maya and from the non-Maya as he was becoming visible in the communities.

Ernesto really came out as a visionary leader. In the beginning he saw the need for the education of his community. He took up the challenge to prepare himself and became the first teacher in his community. He was able to lay a solid foundation for the future of St. Jude R.C. school that is now doing so well under his brother Liberato Saqui. Another vision was his support for the Cockscomb Basin Wildlife Sanctuary. He saw the economic viability for a project that would and could generate income for his people. He pushed it, worked with the women, and encouraged them to establish the craft center. Somebody burned it down but that did not stop them. They bounced back. There is now a bigger market not only for his village, but those of other communities. That indicated an inclusive leader, there was always a selflessness in Ernesto. From time to time that selflessness surfaced as he related to others.

Publishing this book of Ernesto Saqui as a leader is timely as the Maya people are now better identifying themselves as Maya, and feeling more confident as they assert their Mayahood into their independent beliefs. This is even more important after the victories of the Maya Alliance and with the Caribbean Court of Justice (CCJ), which ruled against the Belize government for meddling with Maya land. Now the CCJ insists that the Belize Government needs to do more to identify their properties. These victories have brought more confidence to the Maya leaders. More important than that, the Maya are identified as gifted with their own customary rights that are not represented in the Constitution of Belize. The Government of Belize must incorporate those rights into the Constitution of Belize. Ernesto as a leader can play a big role as that unfolds.

Fabian Cayetano
Barranco Village
November 25, 2019

Foreword II
Ernesto Saqui: An Inspiration

It is a great honour to share a few words about my friend, Ernesto Saqui. I remember meeting him for the first time in September 1990. I was fresh out of college at the time and had just started working with the Belize Audubon Society. I was put in charge to oversee the management of the various national parks and reserves, including Cockscomb Basin Wildlife Sanctuary. I was entrusted with a huge responsibility yet I barely knew my country at the time! Coming from northern Belize and having not previously had the chance to visit the other parts of Belize, I knew very little about other places, cultures and practices other than from what I read in books and newspapers.

Here I was — this young Maya Mestizo man from a northern town meeting a young Maya Mopan man from southern Belize, but not any young man at that. There was something about Ernesto that mystified me. Even in my inexperience I knew this was someone who had already experienced hardships and challenges, and was the wiser as a result.

Yes, Ernesto struck me as a wise man from the first time I met him. He had an aura. He exuded leadership and had a self-confidence about him that I had never seen before. I was technically his supervisor but he was clearly my superior in more ways than one. As his book so vividly portrays, Ernesto had already gone through many trials and tribulations in his life before I met him. Those experiences, and the ones that followed, shaped him into the Maya leader he is today.

I am so happy Ernesto decided to write this book. *Ernesto Saqui Maya Leader* offers fascinating insights into the life that Ernesto has lived. As he describes, life experiences shape a person into who they will be or not be. In the 30 years I have known him, I never really understood what life experiences shaped Ernesto into the person he is until I read his book. I am no longer mystified, but now I am awed.

Ernesto Saqui Maya Leader gives us a glimpse into the lives of a group of Maya people in southern Belize, their hardships and triumphs, their hopes and aspirations. Throughout it all, Ernesto is at the center of it. By the time I met him, Ernesto was already a leader of his people, the founder of a village, an aspiring politician, and the manager of the world's first jaguar preserve.

A man of few words, the book is written in Ernesto's simple and straightforward way. This reminds me of another of Ernesto's characteristics – he speaks in a calm manner and has a very peaceful demeanour. He writes in the same way. Many people initially underestimate or disregard him but eventually realize that he is no push over. To the contrary, Ernesto has the natural ability to figure out a person from the first encounter. Like a master chess player, he is steps ahead of most people who engage him and, as a result, usually has the advantage in discussions and arguments. This skill has served him well with his community and in his private life.

I am pleased to know that Ernesto is still very much involved in the cultural development of his community. As a community leader, and now as an Elder among his people, Ernesto has always been dedicated to "knowing who we are" — never losing sight of who the Maya are. Juuntulico'on is his effort to help his people move forward together via Maya cultural research, awareness and building unity.

Ernesto Saqui: Maya Leader should be made compulsory reading in all primary schools and high schools in Belize. Doing so will expose students from all over the country to a culture that they likely know very little about. It will also inspire many young Belizean students to strive for greatness in the same way that Ernesto Saqui struggled for the well-being of his people.

Osmany Salas
Orange Walk Town
March 19, 2020

xi

Saqui Family in 2011 with parents (*front*), Juana Sho Saqui and Pedro Saqui. (*back from left*) Josepha, Claudia, Frederica, Ernesto, Julio, Liberato, Hermalindo, Narciso, Pio, and Cipriano. Photo courtesy Pio Saqui

Chapter 1
Childhood

Family History

I was born in San Antonio, Toledo, Belize, on November 7th, 1958. My parents are Pedro Saqui and Juana Sho Saqui. My mother's parents were Juana and Daniel Sho. They had both died before I was born.

My father's parents had also died before I was born. In fact, my father was almost an orphan. My father's is a sad story; he had no parents. His father died when he was very young; and his mother died when he was 15 years old. So he went to stay with my mother's family because he wanted my mother as his wife. They took pity on him and allowed him to stay with them. Eventually they allowed him to have their daughter as his wife. She was the last child of ten children, the baby.

All of these people came from San Luis, Peten, Guatemala. The Maya people from this area were being forced to work on the Pan American Highway. They did not believe in forced labor so they escaped this harsh labor by relocating to a distant place where the abusers will not be able to find them ever again. They came together and planned to leave in the dark of the night with all their belongings. They also realized they needed to bring along their two saints, San Antonio and San Luis Rey, and the bell so that their new home would be complete.

They came in the 1880s and settled in San Antonio. They built a church and school. The village has grown to a big village. As far as I know, my parents grew up in San Antonio. That's where the family evolved.

My parents had ten children. Josepha Saqui is oldest, Ernesto, Hermalindo, Narciso, Liberato, Claudia, Julio, Pio, Cipriano, and Frederica. The first eight of us were born in San Antonio and the other two were born in Maya Centre.

San Luis Rey Roman Catholic Church in San Antonio showing bell tower

Memories of Church

I always looked up to my church, San Luis Rey Roman Catholic Church. My family, my other brothers were always very close to church, so we attended the church services. We felt that is the way to start. As children, that is what we believed. I usually went to ring the bell for daily mass and Sunday mass.

That bell was brought to San Antonio from San Luis. The story is that when the settlers were first in San Antonio nothing was going right. Crops were failing, people were sick. They felt that without the saint the village was never going to be a prosperous community. So they went back to San Luis after midnight and got the two saints, San Antonio and San Luis, and the bell. While the village was called San Antonio, to make it more vivid, they called the church and school "San Luis Rey."

Deer Dance, San Antonio, 1989

When that glorious bell rang every day it reminded us of our life everlasting in San Antonio. Every year we had the Deer Dance on the 25th of August to commemorate the establishment of the village. It was beautiful; it was something that was so down

Saqui Family in front of San Luis Rey Roman Catholic Church in San Antonio

to earth culturally and the people had the greatest reverence and respect for it.

I helped the priest give out sweets and the cards that have the picture of Saint Joseph or Saint Anthony or the Virgin Mary as a gift for those who attended church. I have always remembered those as important, so I took that as a great responsibility.

I also helped pump the water for the priest so he had water for the day. I got little awards like little biscuits at the end of the job. I felt strongly that I was doing what most children would not do.

That was in the mid-1960s. Father Jack Ruoff, S.J., always went in his Mini-Mo, a little jeep that he drove to go around to the villages. Father Callistus Cayetano (Father Cal) was always a good priest. He always spoke with the authority of the church to remind you that you are supposed to be a Christian person and we tried to be good. Every member of San Antonio was Catholic and had to go to church and do confession. They participated fully and blended it with their culture. All of the feast days and Holy Week had the greatest meaning for us. It touched so much of our life that we felt that we were living that experience so many years ago. I feel that I was fortunate enough to be part of it. Then I could see the meaning of the church as opposed to what it is now as it has a lesser meaning because there are a lot of other challenges.

San Antonio was once the hope of the priests. I remember when they used to live there as I was growing up. From 1965 when I started school, I went through all the way to Standard VI. I enjoyed those childhood days, getting involved in all the school activities and the church. I played football for the school. It was a great time for me and I have always felt touched by that moment in my life.

Family Life

When I was very young, I used to always do cultural things with my parents. My father did fiestas in July, three in a row. I think one was the Feast of Concepcion. They had novenas that consisted of music, marimba, harp, and dancing. We went to church and brought the saint to go visiting from house to house. I used to love to ring the bell in the procession. I always looked forward to going from house to house and offering gifts in the form of food. Then we went back to the house where there was an altar that was prepared for the saint. Then everybody went to church for the Mass and that was the end of that fiesta. That is what I have learned to appreciate as cultural practices. It is not only fun, but sharing your experience and faith, looking out for food as a gift, ringing the bell. My father did those three times, people coming to our house to make food in preparation, lots of experiences that made it a wonderful moment in my life.

Planting Corn

We didn't plant corn to sell, but we planted it to eat. We only ate what we grew, fresh from the plantation. When it was time to plant corn, there was a cultural preparation for the planting season. My father would find ten men to help plant because the whole plantation had to be planted in one day. He had to decide what kind of corn he was going to plant: white, yellow, red.

He had to discuss it with my mother, because to plant corn, she would have to feed all those people who helped plant the corn. That usually meant preparing pork for Posh or with tortilla. My mother asked the women she wanted to help her for that day so the food would be ready to eat on time at the plantation. Special drinks also had to be prepared. The night before the planting, my father brought three to four men to kill the pig and prepare all the parts for the main meal the next day.

The men played a divination game the night before planting. Four men were chosen because of their outstanding character and standing to play the game. They made a straight line of 30 to 60 corn kernels on the ground. They took the insides out of four kernels and marked them with charcoal. They represent the two solstices and the two equinoxes, the earth/sun relationship broken into four pieces. Each of the four players had a stick or a different colored kernel of corn to mark their place. These four marked kernels were shaken and thrown on the ground. The number of upright ones with the charcoal showing was that person's move, the number of places on the line of kernels that player moved. That was repeated many times as each took their turn, until someone reached the end of the line of kernels. If the person doing the planting tomorrow did not reach first, he would not have a good crop. He would have to do a ceremony for planting, go to the farm and burn copal in the center of the farm, with an invocation to ask for a good crop.

Rice Farming

While most of the food we ate was grown fresh in the plantations, most of our family's income came from rice and beans. The rice was grown farther away, more than three miles near Blue Creek. When my father was cutting rice, around September or October, when the rice is in season, he couldn't come home and go back every day because it was too far. Once the rice was ripe, when you cut it you could not leave it out to get wet. You had to finish the shelling job that day. A sheller was used to thrash the rice bundles so that the kernels fell down and the trash stayed up. He stayed there until he finished the harvest.

My sister Josepha and I were responsible for taking food to my father and his workers. My mother got up very early in the morning to make food for five or six days. She prepared tortillas that were thin like biscuits so they would last awhile. We had to leave early in the morning to walk from San Antonio through Mafredie to Blue Creek. It was a long walk around, or we could go through the mountains, a climb straight up the mountain side. Since it was shorter, sometimes we went on that route.

Because we were young, I was about eight and my sister was ten, we were fearful in the mountain forest. She had confidence in me, because she thought I could take care of her, but I had confidence in her because she was older. My mother said we had to pray to make sure we were safe. We were afraid of all these things we had heard about: ixtabai, yorona, sisimito (a big hairy guy), gigante (a giant), tata duende (forest imp). We did not see any of those things, but we did see lots of animals. At times we saw snakes, agoutis, howler monkeys, but once we saw them it was OK. We could handle it without being fearful. We always went fast and we were happy when we got to the dirt road that led to the farm. Luckily we never had any experience that was difficult to manage. Once we got to where my father was, he had to stock this food, whatever he would use right away, and store sugar, beans, rice, fruits so he and the workers could cook their own food. My sister and I stayed to help the rest of the day and came home the next day.

We grew two types of rice. Blue bonnet rice was ready to reap in September. Another type of rice was "Texas", which was not ready until October.

Once the rice was all bagged, my father brought it in 30 to 60 bags to San Antonio. Then my mother found other ladies to come and help clean the rice. Rice is in a bunch until the grain drops, but the rice is not shelled, that is what is bagged. The ladies went through it to clean it, cleaning maybe five or six bags a day, until 30 to 60 bags were done. Starting with 30 bags, when they were finished, only 25 bags were left as the shells were discarded.

Then my father decided it was time to sell the rice. In those days that was a rare chance to go to Punta Gorda. He had to decide who was going to go. My mother always went and sometimes a few of the children. Sometimes we locked the house and everyone went. We went either Saturday or Wednesday, on a market day. He had to tell the truck the day before that we wanted to go the next day because they came the night before and stacked the rice in the truck. We were excited to go and enjoy ourselves. On the market day, the truck left at 3 am, so we had to get up at 2 30.

The Marketing Board in Punta Gorda put the rice on a big scale to weight it. They paid $25 per 100 pounds if the grain was properly dried. They had a way of testing that. They gave you a paper and you went to the Treasury at the Courthouse to get your money. That made people really feel good about their work. In those days the men decided how the money would be spent, and the women just followed. That was how life as a family worked to stay together.

The first thing the men thought about was that they want to drink rum. My father would buy his rum, but I would get a pair of shoes and a pair of pants for me and my sister, because they knew we had worked hard for this money bringing the food to the men working to harvest the rice. They had to buy soap, kerosene, and some flour, but not a lot, because we grew all our own food.

One time was great because it was time to buy a record player. My sister thought something might happen, she was excited. Ms. Chinda, a Guatemala woman sold a lot of records. They would be playing the records and people lined up with everyone listening. Anyone who wanted that record raised their hand. My father bought a big record player that could play really loud. My parents told us we had to take care of this thing. You work hard and this is the reward.

My mother said before we go home we should get some fishes. The people from Barranco were there selling some nice snappers at 25 cents for a string.

We had to pick up bags to replace the ones we brought the rice in for the next trip. We did that and then mother bought some nice white bread, and a huge, round loaf of sweet bread. Then we all got some lemonade, not Coke in those days, but lemonade. By this time my father was a little drunk because he had been drinking his rum. The truck to go back home left about 1 pm, and we reached home around 3 pm.

My father played the record player really loud while my mother prepared the fish caldo. That was a happy moment when we all sat at the table to eat. My father always tried to do the little things that would make us all happy. After we finished eating, everyone would be asleep by 10 pm. The next day we continued to go to school, and my father went back to his farm for the next harvest of rice. In November they planted a second crop of corn that would be ready in February.

All that was leading to Christmas. They planted beans on September 8th or 15th at the latest, so there would be young beans ready to pick by November first and dry by the end of November. That is because we needed the young beans for the Christmas celebration. They planted a lot of beans so they would have six or seven bags. They brought more money than the rice, which added to the spirit of Christmas because it was the last money that we got before Christmas. This was the happiness of working together.

My Training

My family was big, 12 of us. I don't know how they found the time to clean us, to feed us. There were a lot of boys and we were loud. My mother was never soft. She made a lot of noise, too. We all ate together at the table. Even when some of us started to get married, we were still working together. In evening we still all came together to tell stories. That is how we have always been able to live.

It was never boring. My life was always an adventure. If I did not go with my father to Blue Creek, I went with my mother for corn or firewood, which was closer. My father was never at home doing nothing. I learned what it takes to make a family. That was how he expected us to live. I often filled in whenever he was not around, until I was out of school. I enjoyed that village life.

My father started to take me to the bush when I was five years old. He taught me how to shoot animals for food, to go fishing, to hunt at night, which snakes were dangerous, which animals we could eat, which plants we could eat. All of that allows me to live a rural life. Even now if we don't have something, I can always use the forest. As the head of the house, he had to teach the boys. When we were finished with primary school we need to know how to make a plantation. Then we could get a wife. He was preparing us for the rural life. That is how I would live, to make my farm and make my life. It was the training we got.

He taught me to sharpen a machete and use it properly, to cut away from myself so I wouldn't get hurt. He taught me how to chop with an axe to cut the big trees, to make a wedge so the tree would fall the way you wanted it and not hurt anyone. He taught us to gather firewood. That was very important because how else would my mother make our food? My mother always asked if the firewood was there. We had to have firewood.

We had to have corn all the time, too. But in the event that there was no corn, they would leave one bag of rice. Our task was to clean the rice, to remove the shell by beating it with a wooden pestle. We beat the rice until all the kernels were shelled and we were left with only clean ones. We fanned it to separate the kernels from the trash. If we didn't have corn, we ate rice. It wasn't like today when you could go to the shop and buy bread. They did not believe in buying food. Food comes fresh from the plantation. If there was no more corn or firewood, I would have to run after school to get corn or firewood. If we did not have food in the house, there were other things we could do.

Sometimes my father said "let's go fishing," and we went all the way to Agua Caliente. Those were moments when I was pulling all those fish, it gave me a great fulfillment. When I set out to do something, saw the outcome, it made me feel so great. When I got home, the family made it even more delightful because we had food and it was an indigenous family who sat and ate together.

Bird Trap

This is a trap for small birds, like the White-tipped Dove and Little Tinnamou, that we like to eat. We looked for secondary forest where there are animals and birds looking for food. Without having a gun, we set up these traps to capture small birds. First we cleared the place and looked for sticks about two inches in diameter. We

cut the sticks to about 12 inches long. We made a box by piling the sticks, one on top of the other, about four inches high and across the top, with a little distance between the sticks.

We tied strings to the two corners. We partially broke a stick about eight or ten inches long and passed the string through the stick a little off the ground. We put corn under the string. The bird will come and step on the string, which will break the stick so the box will come down on the bird. We went somewhere for the day and left the trap alone, but we checked it before the end of the day and pulled the trap down over night. After catching a bird, we took the bird away from the trap to clean it somewhere else. We don't want to leave any feathers by the trap.

Usually we set several traps, and we would catch three or four birds for the day, enough to feed our family. We roasted the bird a bit and then made a nice soup, adding jippy jappa and a pepper. That life was very rewarding. All of our family enjoyed that. My father trapped these small birds when we didn't have other food or money.

Ground Mole Trap

The tunnel made underground by the ground mole is visible as a pile of earth above ground. Usually they are found in plantations because they like to eat the plantain sucker, and the roots of corn or jams. The ground mole is trapped for two reasons, to stop them from eating the plants and we like to eat it.

To build a ground mole trap, the direction of the tunnel must be determined. The tunnel is opened about four inches square. A stick is passed in the ground under the tunnel with a string tied to the stick in the centre of the tunnel. Four inches before the stick according to the direction the mole will be going, we buried a wire that came up a foot beside the tunnel. We got a four-foot long stick and stuck it in the ground about a foot and a half in front of the tunnel beyond the wire. We bent that stick back over the tunnel and tied the string to it to pull it down to the ground. The wire was tied to the same long stick. We pushed two sticks on either side of the wire in the ground above the tunnel, high enough so the animal could pass under them. Then we took a hooked stick and put it into the ground away from the tunnel to hold the two sticks down. We used waha or jippy jappa leaf and mud to cover the tunnel to seal it so there is no light that can be seen in the tunnel. Before leaving, we made sure this was all sealed with no light, but then we opened the far end to give light, so the mole would run in toward the light to seal it. The string would be in his way, so he would cut the string, which would make the curved stick fly up and pull the wire up, catching the mole between the wire and the two sticks, which would kill the mole. If the mole escaped, then we knew he was a tricky one, so the next time we set the trap, we put basket tie-tie prickle in front of the string to prevent the mole from escaping.

We set the traps for half a day, went somewhere else, and then checked it before we went home. The next morning, we checked it. Most of the time we caught a mole. If we set several traps, we would catch several. We cleaned them and put them on the fire to roast. My mother decided whether she would made two or three meals out of them. The idea was to have a supply of food for the family. She added green plantain and chocho. We usually ate them with tortilla. We also ate the guts, a special dish for us. We squeezed out the intestines and also included the lungs and heart. We put the guts in a waha leaf with cowfoot leaf, ix pacha, and steamed it.

Fishing Vine

Two plants available in the forest are used for fishing, a shrub that does not grow very tall, like eight meters, and a vine. The vine knocks out more fish than the shrub. To fish with this vine, we took along six or seven men. We located a part of the river where we were going to fish. We cut cohune stalks and built a wall from one side of the river to the other side so that nothing could pass from one side of the wall to the other. We also made another wall upstream. Everything between the walls belonged to us. We went to the forest to cut the fishing vine and bundled them. Once all the vines were at the river, we beat the vines on a rock and soaked them in the river. When we had enough, the fish would be stunned, and come up to the surface of the river on their sides, all sorts of fish, even snake fish. We collected the fish. Once we had enough, we took the vine out of the river and took both ends of the wall out. That neutralized the water so the fish could survive and become normal again.

That is easier than fishing by the line. The problem is that if we put too much in the water we can kill too many fish. These days it is illegal to fish with the vine unless you get a permit from the Forest Department. They give permits with restrictions.

It is possible to catch smaller fishes using the other plant, a shrub with a compound leaf. We took the leaf and mashed it like the vine. The fish become drunk. We could only do this in small streams because it is not as strong as the vine. We also get shrimp. We pick whatever is there. We might get one serving of these fish. We did this on a Sunday as recreation.

Eating these fish never makes anyone sick. We are careful not to use too much of the shrub or the vine, just to knock out the fish. This is something we Mayans do when searching for food, using different techniques.

Thatching a House

My father prepared me for becoming an adult. He said to make sure that I am well prepared to take care of the family. By making that commitment, I must be able to take care of anything that comes in life. First, I had to have a house. We have a connection with the forest, the forest complements us as rainforest people. I must prepare my house. I might not have money to buy materials, but the forest provides. I have to use my knowledge that my parents have provided.

I could not just pick up any tree for the posts. They have to be durable, such as cortez, zapote, or billy web, all hard woods. I looked for the sticks that were good for the frame. The house has to be strong in case of a storm. The next thing was to decide whether to use cohune leaf, or bay leaf. I decided on cohune leaf because it was more abundant and cheaper. The roof must have an A shape. I needed to know how many leaves would be needed. I set a day, found men to help me, and prepared everything. It took three to four days to put up the frame. Because it was family business, my father got the men to help and my mother got the women to help in the kitchen. Support was "I help you and you help me." Women made the food, while the men put up the frame. It was a community thing.

For a house that was eight fathoms long and four fathoms wide, I would need about 400 leaves of cohune. Ten men each cut 40 leaves, or I would have to cut 400 leaves. By using support, the job becomes lighter. That is how we work communally. Only the mature leaves would work. They should be cut three or four days after the full moon. Then there will be fewer wood weevils. The leaf will have a longer life span before it has to be changed. All of the men take a day to split the leaves.

Then it takes a day to thatch a house. The house is measured in fathoms which is the distance between two outstretched arms. This house will be eight by four fathoms with ten rafters on each side. The pitch is measured from the center top to the outside edge. The pitch of this house is three fathoms. The pitch is very important because if it is too low, the house will leak. The decision of which side to do first depends on the sun.

Each of the rafters has a hooked stick sitting on the ground to where the thatching will begin. That is needed to hold up the leaves because everyone has to weave at the same time. It has to be woven properly or it will not work. For this house there are four cross beams attached to the lowest runners that run the length of the house. Round sticks or boards are put on top of the beams for the men thatching to stand on. As the thatching proceeds upwards, those standing sticks or boards are moved to the secondary beams that are attached to runners halfway up.

Ten men stand on the standing sticks so they will be able to weave. We start on the bottom and go up. One bundle is eight half leaves. We send up the first bundle, which is tied to the runner at the lower end of each rafter. This is the first runner on the bottom that is extended out so the rain will not come in. They will tie the whole bundle of eight on the first runner. All ten hooked sticks are moved so the hook is at the second runner. The two men on the ground send up two leaves always groove side up. The leaves go on the outside of the original bundle on the first runner and on the outside of the rafters. Each leaf has a "head" the lower end where the leaf was cut from the tree and a "tip" of the leaf. If the first two leaves are oriented with the head to the far right and the tip in the center, the second leaf will have the head overlapping the tip of the first leaf and the tip of the second leaf to the far left. The next two leaves will have the opposite orientation with the tips to the right and the heads to left, changing to the opposite orientation with each set of two leaves. Two bundles are sent up before any tying takes place.

Either tie-tie could be used from the forest, or tying wire from the shop could be used for tying. It is important to use the tie-tie for the cultural consistency. The tie-tie is collected from the forest. The tie-tie should be dried for at least three days so it won't break when weaving. We need 15 rolls of tie-tie. Each roll has five lengths of tie. Each length of tie-tie could be 15 to 18 feet. Once it has dried, it is ready to use. Each rafter has a tie-tie tied just above the bundle that was tied to the first runner. The tie-tie goes under the leaves from inside of the house to the outside and pulled through to the outside and then brought inside over the top of all the leaves.

The first leaves are moved up the rafter about four inches and the second leaf is moved up the rafter about eight inches. The third and fourth leaves are also moved up the rafter about four inches. Then the tie-tie is moved around the third and fourth leaves, wrapped around the rafter, and pulled as tight as can be. The fifth and sixth leave are moved up about eight inches and the tie-tie moved around them and the rafter, and pulled tight. The seventh and eighth leaves are moved up about twelve inches, the tie-tie pulled around them and the rafter, and pulled tight. The hooked stick is moved on top of the last tied leaves. The next bundle is tied in the same way above the last tie. The process is repeated until it reaches the top. The other side is done in the same way.

To complete the top, we need five pieces of hard stick about one fathom long for the two ends, the middle and one in between on each half, each put through on top of the last leaves. Five men are on top of the ridge facing the same direction. The same two men are handing leaves, but these leaves are not split. The leaves are laid two on each side and two in the middle, and repeated until all except six leaves are used, probably at least 34 leaves. The last six leaves are laid grooves down. Before tying, hand the men four long sticks joined in the middle. Using the tie-ties that are already on the rafters, they tie one end of the stick looping across to the other end until the length of the tie-tie is finished. Now all the leaves are tied. The men push the two sticks on top as far as the end of ties on each side. Then everyone comes down.

My Uncle Benito Choc

Where we lived was very rural. Sometimes what you experience makes sense only because it was rural. My uncle Benito Choc was a healer. He could take care of any problem, whether it was a woman or a man. He was very knowledgeable and kind.

One day when I was about 10 years old, I went to visit him. When I reached, he was in his hammock and he was drinking chicha, a wine made out of corn.

He asked me if I already ate and I said no, but I was not hungry. He started to talk from one thing to the next. He was about 60 years old.

He told me he was going to show me something. He asked me to hand him a piece of the corn husk. He stripped it in seven pieces. He said something, then blew on top of the corn husk pieces and threw them on the ground. Everything started to move and they were all scorpions. Whenever he moved his hand, they didn't go away. After a while they came together. He blew again and they were corn husks again. How could that happen? He said in the past there were so many things that happened that don't happen now. I didn't go often to his house, so he never taught me anything. To me it was magic. I don't know how to explain it.

Flood in Agua Caliente

I went for a day of fishing with my dad. He was a farmer, but he enjoyed many things. He wanted to go to the Laguna behind Agua Caliente. There are several pieces of the Laguna, the upper reaches of Agua Caliente. I loved what my father loved. He said it is always good for you to know other activities, like hunting and fishing,

We were going fishing. It was rainy season, but we were only going for a one-day trip. We took fishing line. My father took his gun. We went through the same hills that we went through going to Blue Creek, but we went in the opposite direction to Laguna. We left at 3 am. It started raining, sometimes with thunder and lightning. The track we were following had water, so we walked in it. We reached a section with only high forest. We met animals, but before he could shoot, the animal was gone.

We needed fish bait, so we tried to dig in the ground, but we found only water. Finally we found a high hill and got a good amount of worms. We packed them, and then reached the first lagoon area. We went across it to get to the big lagoon. We kept walking through another lagoon. There was more water, so we went around to the other side. Rain started, then stopped. We caught only two fish for the day. The fish were not biting. By 3 pm we decided to stop. When we reached it, that lagoon was a little high, so we swam across. When we reached the lagoon that had only a little water before, it was totally flooded. But my father said that he had a good sense of direction. So we walked and walked and finally got to a certain tree and we found the trail. Finally we reached the junction where we went the different direction from Blue Creek. It was dangerous, but my father found our way. Those experiences were meaningful because those are some of the guiding forces that keep a family together.

Other times when we went in the dry season we could catch a lot of fish: blanco, big one, nice fishes, also the freshwater catfish, and bay snook. By that time they were using the hand line. Later they got nets, which used up the resources in that lagoon. People go there a lot to catch fish.

The Lady of the Mountains

One day our parents left home and left a list of things for my sister and me to do. It included doing laundry. She and I went to the place where she did the laundry at the river. That day the river was flooded and the water was brown and dirty. While she began her washing, I walked away from where she was to another trail that led to the other side of the river. The current was very strong and made a lot of noise. I looked across the river toward the other trail. Suddenly, I saw a lady standing in the flooded river behind a big fig tree staring at me. I took a closer look at the woman. She resembled a woman whom I knew from the village. She had long black hair. Her arms were covered with hair. She was wearing a Mayan blouse and the current was at her waist like she is going to be washed away by the current any minute. I quickly went to get my sister to see this woman. In no time we were back to see this woman but in a glance she disappeared.

When our parents came home, they saw that I got wet and thought we didn't do the right things. My father lashed me, but not my sister. I kept waiting to hear about this lady drowned that I had seen in the river. I started to get sick. By dinner I had a high fever. They started to argue that it was because my father lashed me. By 8 o'clock in the night, I was trembling. When I closed my eyes, I could see this lady coming with this long thing to inject me. By 9 o'clock, I was getting worse. I kept screaming, I was seeing people coming at me with needles to inject me.

My father went on his horse to the village to get my uncle. When they reached, the healer said my spirit had been taken away when I was alone. My mother explained what had happened. My uncle did the spiritual prayer on me. Then he did a ceremony like an exorcism. He asked my mother to bring a young chicken, a chick. He cut off the head and spread the chick's blood all around me. After a half an hour, all that screaming stopped. My uncle did another spiritual healing, which he had to do three times before midnight. As soon as he finished the first time, I went fast asleep like dead. At 4 am, the crow of the rooster was so loud that it woke me up. I didn't feel afraid any more. They were all crying around me. My father came to me and said I should never have lashed you and I will never do it again.

This lady was the owner of the mountains. If I had died she would have been successful in taking me away. Using the herbal medicine, spiritual prayer, conducting the rite with the baby chicken, that was feeding of spirit so the spirt could let go of me, an offering instead of taking me. They did a blessing to empower and protect me, to protect me if that lady saw me again. I still feel like I am protected. There is nothing I feel afraid of in the forest. I feel strong when it comes to a spiritual attack. When you are trying to do good, it is hard for anyone to attack you.

Maya culture is full of a lot of myths. While we were setting up our traps, or any activity in the forest, such as hunting or fishing, we were told to be careful in the forest. While it is important to do all of these activities, we were interfering with the life out there in the forest. There were always a lot of consequences, a tree could drop on you, you could get bit by a snake. Especially when you hear the Squirrel Cuckoo, it is a reminder that something terrible is going to happen. Exercise caution; the moment is full of danger, an animal can attack you, snake bite, if you have a gun, you could accidentally shoot yourself or your partner. When the bird calls, now you have to be very careful. Or if the Squirrel Cuckoo is jumping around on the road where you are going, that is a bad omen.

If an owl comes inside the house, that means someone has put a spell on you through obeah. Take lit firewood and stone that bird with it. That will take away the obeah. Owls like to imitate a baby cry. If an owl is sitting on your house, that indicates there is something wrong, maybe with the baby.

One person had set a trap for birds. He saw birds in the trap, but he heard Squirrel Cuckoo calling. His trap was near the edge of the Bird of Paradise. But there was a snake already interested in the bird in the trap, so he got bit. If you repeat the process of trapping birds too much, it is seen as an abuse of the opportunity to use these resources. That was the consequence when he did not heed the sign that he was trapping birds too much. We have to live within our means. It is only good to do it some of the time. That was a powerful lesson in the use of resources. When we abuse these opportunities, we must reflect, we are taking and taking, especially the birds. To make it normal again, we must go and acknowledge that we have abused the system and ask for forgiveness, saying "I did not mean to hurt the forest, I am very sorry about it. Now I make my offering." Then we will burn incense near a ceiba tree, a cave, or a special place where the owner of the forest might be.

Primary School

I loved to go to school. I admired my teachers. I won the award for penmanship. I was small, but I used to write very pretty cursive writing and the teacher used to give me beautiful stars on my card. As I grew older, I participated in Christmas entertainments. Those were important for me. When I was in Standard IV, V, and VI, I became a team player for football. I always enjoyed the competition with other schools.

I had games with schoolmates, both at school and at home. We always ran after school to the waterfall to swim for an hour and then go home. Our parents hit us for it. We went fishing in the river and caught these cyclids, or bass, as we called them. They were common in those days because there were not very many fishermen. My mother prepared the meal and she loved it. It was never boring. My life was always an adventure. Sometimes my father said "let's go fishing. " And we went all the way to Agua Caliente. Those were moments when I was pulling all those fish, it gave me a great fulfillment. When I set out to do something, saw the outcome, it made me feel so great. When I got home, the family made it even more delightful because we had food and it was an indigenous family who sat and ate together.

My teachers used to select me because I was an open person, always active and involved in different activities. They were fond of me. My best teacher was Mr. E.P. Cayetano, father of Roy Cayetano. He was always strong and stern, but in many ways very polite. He made sure you would think and move in the right direction. I had this experience of enjoyment of school and home. I had my father's encouragement to be a farmer like him. At 14 years I already had my first milpa, right next to his, and he praised me for following in his footsteps.

High School

All of that changed when I went to high school. To my father, I faded away and made a completely different focus than the direction I had been moving. He was disappointed but supportive. He was always very proud of me.

We sat the Entrance Exam to qualify to go to high school. I was very fortunate, I passed it, but I didn't have any money to go to high school. My uncle Elogio Sho was always interested in helping people. I first knew him when I was about 12 years old because he wanted me to go to high school. He had arranged with the priest like a scholarship where I would stay at the Catholic dormitory in town. He said, "You should go to school because education is going to be important to you. Most of us don't have education and that gives us problems sometimes."

Father Jack Ruoff, S.J. decided to give us scholarships to go to St. Peter Claver High School in Punta Gorda. I was so happy when they informed me that I would be given a scholarship to go to higher studies. I felt so proud of myself. The opportunity to move on came, so I went. It was a major step for me, the transition to high school in Punta Gorda. That transformation was a step toward to the next level of education for Maya people who otherwise would stay in the countryside. It is a move that is recognized in the village as success that is accepted. But some Maya people don't think they should send their children to further education that they should stay on the farm. Still they accept that some of us do raise up and move on to the next opportunity that is available.

Since Father Ruoff organized the scholarship for us, they put us in a dormitory. There were about six of us and Father Ruoff looked after us. He found a cook for us. We had to help maintain the yard, pump water, and ring the bell. It was similar to being at home, but it was different because the food was different; the order of things looked different; people thought differently. It was a Garifuna town, so I began to see things differently, a transition experience. Unfortunately I didn't finish there. I did only First Form, my first year, because things changed and I had to leave.

Chapter 2
Moving North

It was in the 1970s that the movement of people started. They moved because there was this idea that the Indian reservation was being sold to some people. We lost the sense of community in San Antonio when they started to divide the land and you could purchase a piece. That is not part of us where we can buy a piece of land, so we left.

My uncle Elogio was the leader in San Antonio, but he moved away from that idea. Instead of moving deeper into the forest, he came toward the center of the country to find opportunities and improve his way of life. Around 1973 he went with a few men to find a place.

He took some family members because he didn't want them to suffer. He asked my parents to come and live in the Stann Creek District, but we didn't want to then. A couple of years later we went and joined him because we are family. He is our true uncle, the brother of our mother, and he looked out for us. It was important for him to do it as the older brother who was looking after his family.

That move caught me at the end of my first year in high school, but I had to go. They were not going to leave me behind; education or no, I had to go. So we moved from the Toledo District to the Stann Creek District, stopping at Mayan Mopan for one year where my uncle first located. But it didn't work out because of distance from the main highway. It was difficult to get services up there and we had some trouble with the people who were there.

The people that we had trouble with were in a place called "Alabama," where the company had a banana industry. So my uncle did not go there, but started a village that he called "Maya Mopan" beside the creek. But there were disturbances with the people from Alabama who felt that we shouldn't be occupying that area because it was all supposed to be for them. My uncle was able to get that piece of land and settled there. But things didn't work out. The people from Alabama actually fought with my uncle and his group. We were not there yet. Only four or five families came with him at first, but there were other people who were already in the area that joined him to make the village of Maya Mopan.

When we got there in late 1975, there was a problem between my uncle and that group of people, the Tush family. They were a family of about seven brothers who were violent and never respected my uncle because he had the ability to establish a place and fight for what is right.

On 10th of September, 1975, we were having a celebration because that was a big day. But that day there was an incident. My uncle had a common-law wife, not his real wife, and she had a son, my uncle's step-son. There was a problem between the step-son and my uncle after the celebration when the step-son nearly killed my uncle. This guy had a big spear-fishing rod and wanted to puncture my uncle straight through to kill him. He had the intention to kill him, but my uncle was prepared and defended himself. The step-son was so drunk that my uncle was able to beat him. In the afternoon around 3 o'clock my uncle ordered us to tie the step-son to the beam under the clinic and watch him until he got sober.

But by one o'clock in the morning the step-son died while we were watching him. We informed my uncle and he told us that we should always give the story as it occurred and we did. The police came and he went to jail for one overnight and then he came back. He was a strong individual and managed to explain himself. His case came up, but he explained that it was self-defense. He was acquitted and that made the case go clear.

But it compounded the problem with the Tush family on the other side of the creek, even though the step-son was not related to the Tushes. After that my uncle decided, "We can't stay here. We need to look for a better place, a place nearer a town with easier access, a place we can call our village."

The latter part of December a group of us walked from Maya Mopan, starting at 3 o'clock in the morning and walked all the way to Kendall. My uncle Elogio Sho, my father Pedro Saqui, Maricio Bolon, Margarito Bolon, Luciano Bolon, Gregorio Sho, and others. Just the men came to scout the area.

We wanted to stay at Kendall, by the river, but there was an old man, a Mr. Reynolds, who said, "No, you can't stay here. You should go to the next creek." That was Cabbage Haul Creek, so we went there. That was December of 1975. We stayed there about a week. We were there for Christmas and five days more. We knew this would be our home.

Beginning of Maya Centre

When we got here, the place was very appealing for us, so we decided this was going to be our home. The first thing we did was build nine huts so families would have somewhere to live. Then we went back to Maya Mopan and brought all of the families that wanted to come. We brought everything, our chickens, our dogs, our horses. Nine families came right here. The village was officially settled January 2, 1976.

When we came here we wanted to make this place our village. We wanted to make sure that whatever we see here will stay with us and we won't have to leave. We decided that we wanted to mold us as a group and that would make us better people in a given community. We wanted our name to identify us as Maya, so we called it "Maya Centre."

We found this land all beautiful and there was nobody around. So we settled here, and started our village. We needed to have a progressive village, but there was nobody to advise us, so we had to create our own kind of system. We had someone to lead us, my late uncle Elogio Sho. We decided he would be the one to lead us.

We wanted to ground ourselves as independent, so no government would be able to move us. We needed two buildings, a church and a school, at that time a Catholic church and a Catholic school. We started with that in mind, and opened the place, cleared the village site for a church, a school, and other public buildings. Around that central area would be the community, the residences.

After 1976, we realized that in making a community like any other community, things must fall in place. After we built the school and the church, where would the people come from, the teacher to teach in the school? We voted and decided that we had to take all that responsibility on ourselves, who will be the teacher? Fortunately I was with them. In 1978 when the school began, I was the teacher selected from among the others. We had to be quick. If we don't do it, we could be driven out. Because of the school and the church it would be difficult for any government to drive us out. We didn't want to have to fight to go anywhere else.

We had a plan, but one year later we were handed a letter saying "you people must find another place to go." We didn't know this land was an estate, the Turton estate. We were twelve families that were committed, that wanted to make sure we could stay here. We discussed this letter, what we should do, are we going to stay? The conclusion was that we stay and we will fight any problem that comes. If we had to take this land by force we would do it.

The man kept coming and saying that you people will have to move, you can't be here. Finally we got the concession that we could stay for awhile, but he said, "Don't plant any permanent crops because you will have to leave soon and we don't want you to have to leave permanent crops behind."

They were beginning to realize that it was going to be difficult to move us. We continued our way of life developing our village. One day Father Howard Oliver, a Catholic priest came. When he came I was teaching. He looked at the situation and looked at us. After the children went to lunch he came and asked me, "Are you a teacher." I said, "Yes, I have to be a teacher; we have to have a teacher." He asked, "Who said you had to have a school and what made you think you could be a good teacher?"

I said, "The circumstances mean that I must be a good teacher." Then he said, "I am the Manager of the Roman Catholic schools in this district, so it is my job to come and visit you. I am very impressed with what you are doing with these children. I didn't know there

Saint Jude Catholic Church in Maya Centre in 2019 (not the original building)

was a school here. I am going to take over some responsibility because I see a great opportunity in this settlement. We will not be able to pay you, but we will eventually find someone to take over this school. Do you have a church?"

I said, "Yes, that building over there is the church." He said, "Let's organize a Mass for another Sunday." So we all came together for the Mass. He encouraged us to work together and continue the village. We felt so good that he came to us and said he would take up the challenge to help us. The sisters came and did different classes.

The next big issue was to ground ourselves and secure the land for the village. There is no way an estate can be ours unless the government came to help us. One day people came who were campaigning. They asked, "How can we help you?" We told them that we needed a piece of land, and to make sure our village is safe. "We would like to find out if we can live in this village."

That was Hon. David McCoy who came. He said, "I will help, but we need your support. When we win, we can get land for you. Rest assured, if we win, you will get your land." It was during the time before Independence, so I don't know what he was called, but equivalent to the Area Representative now.

The election came and they won. Hon. David McCoy came back and told us, "Now we can work. We will not allow your village to go away. We are going to acquire a piece of land from this estate and make it yours."

After the election we kept going back and forth to visit the Premier, the Hon. George Cadle Price and he told us, "if you are good Belizeans, hard-working people, I am prepared to help you." Finally we were informed that they bought 1,000 acres for farming on the other side of the Southern Highway and 50 acres on this side for the village. We knew we were going to be living here and develop our village.

CHAPTER 3
Education and Teaching

I continued high school in Dangriga at Ecumenical. It was difficult for me because the food was different. They only had a light tea in the evening. I woke up hungry in the night. I chopped yards with other families so I had money. I boarded with a Garifuna family. In the rainy season it was all flooded and full of mosquitos. I did my own laundry on the weekends. They told me that my clothes were so clean, smelled nice. I was good at laundry. These outside experiences made me more open.

After I graduated from Ecumenical in 1981, I taught at Independence for a year or two. You had to sit a First Class Teachers's Examination. I passed that exam and then in 1984 and 1985 I was in Teacher's College in Belize City. Before I went to Teacher's College I was on salary teaching in Independence. But whenever I got my salary, I had to share with my father to help my brothers to go to school, so I didn't have a chance to save any money.

I found a place to rent cheaply and thought all was well because I would get the money to pay the rent at the end of the month and I was on salary. Except that the people where I was renting expected the rent in advance and would not let me stay there. I was very worried because I was homeless in Belize City with only my bag on my back. I didn't want to go back home. I couldn't turn back to my parents because I knew they didn't have any money.

But I knew Lynn Fields, a nun at St. Ignatius, so I found her and told her my problem. She said she would pay my rent if I would clean their yard. So I continued cleaning their yard all the time I was in Belize City.

There were many times when I had so many assignments that I had to study by candlelight. When it got to be about 11 pm and I was not yet finished with my work for the next day, they would call to me to turn off the light, because I was burning too much current. I turned off the light and burned candles. There were times when

"

there is no water. She had her tank on the side of the house. I would ask for some water, but she said there wasn't any more. There was another man from Corozal who was staying upstairs, paying more. He used the hot water and everything. I am from the forest. I didn't need hot water.

When I got back to Independence, I did an internship joint with Jamaica and the Belize College of Arts, Science and Technology. The Jamaica people came and did the final exam, supervision of teaching in Independence. They gave you what you were going to teach. I got Standard 3. I did what I needed to do.

I lived with some people from Seine Bight who were very noisy. The priest said, "this is no place for you." They had a house in Mango Creek that I could use. When I got there, I felt like a king. I had my own kitchen.

The Jamaicans asked for my work. They were very hard. In front of my students I was never nervous. I gave the students their work, but the people from Jamaica collected the students' papers to mark them. They said I was not a perfect teacher, but very good. They gave me a B+. I was excited. I was coming to the end of another part of my education.

I graduated in 1985 from Teacher's College which was then a part of the Belize College of Arts, Sciences and Technology (BELCAST). The graduation ceremony was at the Civic Centre in Belize City. We had to pay, but I was not worried. I was teaching so I had money. I couldn't get my parents to come and see me, but my younger brother Liberato came. People asked me, "how old is your father?" The graduation was at 9. There were all the marches and the speeches. The greatest moment for me was when they called my name to walk across to get my diploma. We decided we would not stay in Belize City, so we went straight to the bus to come home. Once we returned, they made some food for us. My family shared in my success. Each one was giving their own idea for what success means. It was a lot of encouragement. Our families look up to each one of us as we attain education. I consider it a great success to reach that level of education.

Teaching in Independence

I continued to teach at Independence. I was offered to be the Principal, but I knew I would not be the Principal. But I took on greater responsibility in that school.

Group trained as Roman Catholic Catechists at Trinidad Farm in the early 1980s.
I am second from the left in the first row.

I was a lay minister and had services for the entire school every Friday. Some people called me Father. Independence has varying morality, lots of problems with youths, women having babies very young. I did a little bit of homily on taking up the way to live, how to respect each other. The Bible became a routine, everyone knows on Fridays the school has a church service. We must make it as down to earth as we can, act like a good example for them. That was important for me to do. When the time came for me to leave, everyone said what would happen to the church service? I had made a good connection with the students, became a people-oriented person. Every time they came for advice, I gave them ideas and they solved their own problems. Even parents came and talked to me. I just told them how I felt about the issue. You become like an advisor, a councillor. All of that came to an end when I left the teaching profession. In the presence of some of the teachers, Father James Short said, "You are not a jaguar-oriented person; you are a people-oriented person. If at any time you want to come back, just let us know."

I volunteered to teach the Teachers who had to pass the second class and first-class exams. I had already been to Teachers' College, so I knew what were in those exams. They gave you an outline of what is expected. So, I helped them after school. We started at 4 pm and then we went home at 5. Sometimes when the teachers passed by for help, I would be cooking. They said men shouldn't be cooking. But I had to help myself.

The School Manager over Independence told me I should be able to take over the school while the Principal was going to training. But the Principal said, "Big man don't go to school," so I figured he would not go to training. I told the local manager to put that on hold. But it was then that I was offered the job as Park Manager of the

Cockscomb Basin Wildlife Sanctuary. The teachers were going to sit the exam in June and July, but I left the first of May, 1987.

Encounter with a Bear

While working as Cockscomb Basin Wildlife Sanctuary Park Director I was given the opportunity for some training in the Pennsylvania, U.S. One aspect was research and I was sent along with another trainee to go with a researcher who was trapping bears. We went to the site where a bear had been caught in a trap and was screaming. The researcher told us to wait to the side until he called for us. He took some of the instruments out of his bag, but left the bag with us.

I asked what to do in case a bear attacks and the answer was totally different from my experience in the rainforest. First we were told what not to do. "Don't run or climb a tree," the two things I would do in case a jaguar was chasing me. "Just stay put and make sure you stay low. But there is no need to be concerned about black bear attack. I have been working for 20 years and there has been no attack. I am going to do my work and then I am going to call for you."

He left most of the equipment. He was going not too far from us. Before he got to the animal he had to bend down to get to the other side. I thought I saw something black and then I heard the splattering of instruments. I thought everything was OK because that is how he does his reserch. I still heard the screaming. Then it was quiet. From a distance we saw this animal pull a pine tree and snap it. Then the animal headed straight for us.

This animal stood on two back feet and was roaring. The animal was circling around us on two legs and then on four legs, but then disappeared. Then she came back from the other direction. We were clapping and screaming. For the third time and she came right up to us. We stooped down and screamed. She went down on four legs and went away. At that point I knew she wasn't going to hurt us.

Then the researcher darted the yearling and loosed it so when it woke up, the yearling could go. He said that we needed to get out of there because the mother might come back. The animal that was screaming was a yearling and the bear was the yearling's mother who was very upset. The researcher got scratched on his back. He was very nervous. Everyone was very quiet. We got to the truck.

I was so happy that nothing happened to me. I know I would be in trouble if I got hurt.

Ernesto Saqui with a bear in Pennsylvania

Chapter 4
Developing Maya Centre
My Uncle My Mentor

When Maya Centre started, the leader was Elogio Sho, my uncle. He was a strong leader and never failed at what he set out to do. We were so happy that we could begin to work. The first set of clearing was where Liberato lives now. The first church and school were where the clinic is now. They were only thatched roof buildings.

My uncle, Elogio Sho, was a visionary, a leader in his own way. For a long time he had been looking after people. If there was a land issue, he tried to solve it so they would have their land. I got to like him because of the ideas he had. He gathered his people, talked to them, and they followed him. In that way he started Maya Mopan.

He started, but never finished; still we were continuing to follow him. He was making people understand how important it is to work together. My uncle was good enough to create the community to share information and support. I was by his side to take notes. It was a great movement; I learned his ways, his planning. There were so many things that we wanted to do together.

There came a time when my uncle's leadership was questioned. A visitor came and he decided to work with that person. He had been a Catholic, but these church people that came to visit him were Baptists. He said he had to move on because there was better hope with them, especially since he wanted to be a preacher man. He started to disagree with the community. There was bickering. Our peaceful community started to break apart, to become disintegrated. We were disappointed. The community broke apart. Some went with him and some stayed with the Catholic. It was a Catholic church that we built, but he opposed it. He tried to close the school and start his own school. But the school was under Roman Catholic management.

This was the time we had to make a decision. We didn't want to be part of the Baptists. We were on the road to developing, why would we want to break apart? We tried to work together, but it never worked. There was even a bad physical encounter. It was time to take leadership to develop the community. We overthrew him at a meeting after forcefully asking him to vacate the leadership position. We wrote the Ministry to come and intervene. They said we needed a by-election in 1985. The solution was that Ignacio Pop, who was a Justice of the Peace, held over for one month, and then there was a by-election.

I was elected Chair of the Village Council. My uncle started to think I wanted to be a leader. I didn't want to take him down. He had started to move anyway. When that day came that I won, he had to understand that he was no longer the leader. He had to understand that I was now the leader. He stayed in the village for awhile and then he moved on to another location near Belmopan. He took some people, but he only got his children and son-in-law to go with him. They wanted to be more like other cultures, not a Maya way of life. The government said there would not be an opportunity for him to start another "problem." They didn't want him to continue to develop a village that would cause a problem for the government. That community was near Armenia. He got sick and died there.

He was someone I admired. He had the ambition and intelligence to make things happen. He knew how to ask for what he wanted, to gain support. When I took over from him I felt I worked along with the community, developing the community. We got a school, health post, community centre, lights, water, and more school buildings.

The first water system was a small tank and it was not enough. Then we got a bigger tank and dug farther down. This is an example of progress, leaders who see the need for people to have a better way of life, a vision of leadership that I learned from my uncle.

Acquiring Land

We realized that we didn't want to keep moving different places. We wanted to make our village successful with each one seeing their way to a better way of life, with our children getting education and better jobs. One issue was land. We wanted to acquire land for the village, 15 acres more for house lots. Through the government, the Village Council got 15 more acres for house lots in addition to the 50 acres previously provided for the village site. In 2007 we acquired another portion, 35 acres for another 124 lots for the village site. It was hard for first owners, but by pooling resources we could negotiate with a land owner. William Bowman said, "If you come up with the money, I will sell you the land, $55,000 for 35 acres." The limit was four parcels per person, because if there was just one per person, we would not have the money to buy. Some people had money more than others, and time was running out. Allowing some to buy four parcels made it work. I tried to encourage them. "God is not making more land," I said.

It is always difficult to get land. We had to sacrifice, and then stay, not resell, or give to someone who is not in the community. When people own land, the problem comes if many sell. That will undermine the purpose. For a long time that was OK, until people got an opportunity to sell. One or two have sold, but most have stayed. I expect them to use their judgment not to sell. We are able to do it on our own. The people have begun to realize that rather than wait for the government, if they can, they do it themselves.

Water

At first we didn't have good drinking water and the community of Maya Centre was really in need of it. Water is life! After we settled in, we had to start with water. We knew water from the creek was not the best. Our first water system was a self-help project. We investigated some form of water system. A Peace Corps project provided three hand pumps. But it didn't provide for everyone's needs because some were far from the pumps.

We were working with that system when United Nations High Commissioner for Refugees (UNHCR) came. We asked them for help in adding a concrete classroom to the school. They said, "Sure, we will provide the materials, but you have to provide the labor." The community was quite happy with that and willing to provide the labour. In designing the building, we were talking about whether to put pipes in the building. But we didn't have a water system, so why would we put in pipes? We asked for help with a water system, but they said since we already had the hand pumps we didn't qualify under their rules.

Finally they agreed that we could have a gravity-fed system. That became a Peace Corps project. We walked upstream along the creek until we found the right place. There we dammed a section of the creek and put up a 1,000 gallon tank. The hydrant pump provided the energy to pump water up into the tank where it was chlorinated. From there the pipes ran to all the lots in the village, but only to the lot, not into the house. Each family had to put in the pipes to get the water from there into the house. That was how we got the first system.

Families still need to pay a small fee, but there were no meters, so everyone paid the same flat fee. With a tank holding only 1,000 gallons, the water was to be used only for drinking and cooking, not for laundry or washing the car. The village was doing well, so more houses were built and the demand for water increased. During the peak, there was no water. Then the pump started breaking down, and we had to get parts and eventually a new pump, but they came from far away, like Thailand. There began to be problems because some people were wetting their nursery farms, and some had large nursery areas. Others who could afford a car, were washing their cars. People said they didn't want to pay when others were using too much water. The solution was put gauges in the water system, but who could help us do that? Help for Progress and Peace Corps.

In 2001 Maya Centre was included in the Rural Communities Rudimentary Water System Project. We had to do a survey on how many people there were and how we were using water. The Horizon 2000 British Army drilled a well. Then the government was going to do the system, but that didn't happen. We borrowed a submersible pump from Rural Development and connected to the first system for distribution of the water, just to see if it would work. That didn't work, so every evening we pumped and people came to fill their containers with water. Eventually the Rudimentary Water project came and finished. They built the towers and laid pipes.

They did not meterize it, so every household just paid $10 per month. Some were accusing others for using too much. In 2004 the Water Board was established. Their job was to change over to a meterized system so everyone could pay for what they use. That was how that started. Monies collected were to establish new pipes or for new families, or to use for other community purposes like to help the school. But they had accumulated. By 2006 all the water system was meterized. For $10 a month, you get 1,000 gallons, and then you pay a few cents per gallon above that. Still there were complaints. Some said water should be free. But there are expenses. The more you do, the more materials are needed, and we had to buy in bulk to have it ready for people. The Village Council encouraged the community to take advantage of the system, but not to abuse it. The education sessions about how it works were very important.

It used to be that if there was a broken pipe, no one cared. But after they understood the system, they knew it mattered because it would make someone pay more.

We started to have serious problems with the water system when the government changed in 2008. Even the three tanks were not enough, because the area was expanded and Kendall was included. The water finished fast and we needed new pipes. The community would have to come up with some money.

Elevated Water Tank

So in 2010 we got a new elevated tower. The three tanks are gone and we have 24-hour service, 20,000 gallons, which cost $225,000. Even Kendall people were included, also the Charles Citrus Farm to the south, and Boman's Emerald Grove to the north of the village. I think we can still manage to add a few more people. It is an OK system now, quite adequate to serve the purpose. Still the demand is high; the farms use a lot of water.

Water is life, but water is one of the hardest things to manage. A community goes through a lot, cutting off for non-payment, making changes in the Board, getting a new chairman. We are clear that our water is our creek. No one should destroy it, clear next to the creek, or pollute it.

Now we have a system that Maya Centre is happy about and there are always extra funds to assist other projects. For the celebration of 21st, the Water Board, Village Council, Women's Group, and PTA, all cut out a bit of their budget to support the celebration. When the school needed assistance, the same organizations came forth with the money to pay for one teacher for the beginners and middle classes. She was good with education, and we were able to put up her salary. Before Christmas, we looked around the village for the elderly who could not buy their clothes, and buy some for them, or anyone else who needed that help.

Electricity

We were aware that without electricity, one would never make it with ease. During the developing stage there were so many things that we wanted all at once. We got the first water system before electricity because the pump was powered by the flow of the stream. But that was not adequate, so the second system had a pump that required electricity.

In 1989 we heard that electricity was going to come to Sittee River and it is close to us. They were nominated as a community to receive electricity, but Maya Centre was not included. We felt like we were being left out. Why should we be waiting when everyone else was getting electricity?

This is what I like about Maya Centre people. We are always ready to do it, no matter what it takes, we can get it done. It only takes a bit of energy to start and it is done. So we went to the meeting and made our argument. We are the last village in this group heading south. When you do the next group, you will skip us and go on to the next village further south. They promised to look into it and a month later they sent a letter saying we had been approved. We were so happy. They signed us up. The day came, they surveyed and told us we had to move the water pipes because they were where the posts would go. They came and put pegs where the posts would be.

But then something went wrong, the money was gone and they stopped before they got to us. We were so disappointed. For the water system we had a borrowed pump that needed electricity, so we borrowed a generator to pump water for containers every evening.

Then 1991 came and they put up only three posts, but in August of 1992, they told us they would turn on the lights, just before the celebrations. Everybody in the community got ready and at 6 pm sharp they turned on the lights. Truly and honestly, a lot of them saw the light at that time. They knew that this would enhance the life and the development in the village. There were speeches about what it would mean to the community. That was only street lights, not electricity to the houses, or to the pump. By November there was electricity to the water pump. Every family had to pay to get it to their house. By Christmas everyone who could afford it had light in their houses.

From the three posts it expanded quickly. I pushed the Minister to get electricity here to my place and he agreed without coming to see. When he saw how far it was, he said it cost a lot to do it, but look at all the development that has come to this area.

Electrification brought a new vision. It gave us a lot of hope. Maya Centre is fortunate because they use digital things for the restaurants and other businesses, for students. It is really helping the village. There is no need to go to town to do anything. It empowers us, because we jumped on it. When we see something, it happens. That is how the community likes to move. The community not only took advantage of it, one way, but other ways, too. They use electrical tools, which helps the little man build his house. The cost is there, but they understand that they have to pay. Electricity is power. It helps with everything. Now we are so dependent on electricity that when it goes dark, we don't know what to do. Cable Internet is also available in the village. It is so much easier to do everything here. Students come here to use our Internet instead of going to Dangriga. All of this came about because we had this vision of having electricity. We are happy that we were able to do it because there are a lot of benefits to having done it.

CHAPTER 5
Cockscomb Basin Wildlife Sanctuary

If it didn't work for us to live in Maya Centre, we really wanted to live in Cockscomb. There were some who attempted to go to live in Quam Bank, but they were asked to come back. We continued to develop this community for those of us who wanted to stay and work together. We rediscovered ourselves. At first we thought we would make it on subsistence farming. Then we attempted citrus, which was good only for a while. It got very difficult for small famers when the Citrus Growers Association instituted mandatory new standards to control the disease called "greening." The spraying itself had to be done three times a year, each time costing nearly $100 per acre. You can cover your trees with a tent to get rid of the greening, but who can afford a tent for every tree? When a field is abandoned, by law you have to cut down the trees and burn to control the greening. Most Maya Centre farmers have abandoned citrus because they cannot afford to meet the new standards.

The conservation of the jaguar reserve changed the way we do things. It was the hope we didn't expect. When it came, at first we were not in agreement. We felt it was someone else's paradise and we should have nothing to do with it. We thought something was being taken away from us. People said, "Let's fight this Cockscomb." But they went back and forth, why now, why not before? I wondered where we were on this. I was still a teacher, but I knew the problem.

When I was given the opportunity to work in Cockscomb in 1987, all these things came together. Daniel Taylor was the Peace Corps worker in the Sanctuary. One day the community had a plan was going to grab Dan Taylor and beat him. They told me about it, not realizing the BAS was already looking at the situation. Dan Taylor came to see me and said we need a Belizean with good leadership to lead the Sanctuary and we were thinking about you. I was a little disappointed because I loved my job as a teacher.

Before I made any decision, I needed advice. I went to my local school manager, who said you are secure as a teacher. If you want to take the new job, take a leave for two years. Then if you don't like it, you can come back as a teacher. When Bishop Martin came for Confirmation in the village, he asked me how was my teaching. I said, "very well, but I might quit teaching and go into conservation. He said, "you are not a jaguar-oriented person. You should stay in the classroom."

But I felt good that they had asked me to take that leadership, so in May of 1987 I took the position of Park Director of the Cockscomb Basin Wildlife Sanctuary. The whole community was against me, saying that I should not have gone on the side of the enemy. But I had a reason. If we were to continue the way we were, it would not work. I wanted to change feelings of hate to those of development. I wanted to make opportunities for the people of Maya Centre. The Belize Audubon Society told me that that they wanted me to encourage the community to understand the reason for the establishment of the Sanctuary and to lessen the hatred.

(*from left*) Alfonso Ical, Ernesto Saqui, Ignacio Pop, Hermelindo Saqui

I used my uncle's strategies working with the people. I rang the bell and called a meeting of the people. I told them we had a choice to make, either work with Cockscomb, or forever have the fighting. Maybe there will be opportsunities for us. But they only wanted to talk about fighting to get rid of those people, so they left.

That gave me an idea of the new challenges ahead. I left it for awhile. The next time I invited only the women and said to them, "We understand there is a problem with Cockscomb. Here is what I am thinking. I want us to work with Cockscomb in a way that we can all benefit. We started to think what we could do. We are Maya people, people want to know us. We are very artistic people, doing embroidery, clay beads. Maybe they will like our work.

The women said, "If you truly believe that this will work, let us try it. It will not be like before, we will have new ways of doing and being."

"Go back to your houses, and do your best work. In the evening, think about what you can do with your hands. Come back in two months and we will see what we have done," I told them. I thought they saw what I was trying to do.

After two months they came, bringing whatever they made. We had two tables, one on each side, table 1 and table 2. I told them to take a look at whatever items you have done. If you think it is pretty, put it on table 1, not so good on table 2. It is going to be important because these items speak of us, of what we are worth. I made them think.

It was a good meeting, cordial. We were talking about what we were going to do with products like these. We decided we will have collective decisions. Whatever we do, we will do it together so that others can learn. When you come back to the next meeting, bring more stuff. Two months later we had another meeting, and they had become innovative and enjoyed their crafts. Several months passed and we had five meetings already. In addition to making the crafts, the women began to talk about putting up a little house where we could sell. They said, "how do we build this building? We can't do it because we are women." But some said, "I will tell my husband. We can make a schedule, and the men can cut material and build.

In the meantime, Ignacio Pop and his son Pedro were the wardens working for the Belize Audubon Society (BAS) that was managing the Cockscomb Basin Wildlife Sanctuary, so Ignacio put the gate on the road in front of his house. He and his relatives were selling in front of his house. Tourists were buying through the car windows. Even children were selling clay beads they had made. The *Boston Globe Magazine* called it "clay bead city." But it was beginning to be a problem. The children didn't want to go to school. Only one family was benefitting. The larger community said, "why is this happening? We said we were going to do this together."

I went to BAS, asked them in the interest of building a relationship with the community, would they consider moving the gate and putting it in a neutral place in the village. At first the reaction was not too cordial. The BAS Executive Director, Micky Craig said,"what would happen if it didn't work? It would be too difficult because it would be too people oriented. Although the Belize Audubon Society works with community groups, we are not a community organization; we don't fund groups." The President, Victor Gonzalez, mentioned to me that he thought it was "a damn good idea," but he advised me to leave it for another day.

So I left and came back to the village worried. There was a Village meeting about building the structure, and that started to happen. I was amazed at the interest of the women, what they were willing to put up with it, and I was happy for that. After the completion of the structure, I went back to BAS and told them again why we would want to put the gate there. I showed how we want to work together with BAS and this will be communication between the two. It will give the women a chance to feel some ownership of the jaguar preserve. Both parties will be successful and benefit together. This time BAS said, "Let's do it, but if anything goes wrong you will be responsible to correct it."

I quickly put my act together. We built 18 shelves for stalls for 18 women. We had a drawing with corn red, black, and green to decide who would get what stall. They put all those items that they made, and decided the prices they would charge. Finally they decided the group who would run the show. I said we needed five beautiful, colourful women in traditional Mayan dress, to run the place. Those were the people responsible for selling the crafts.

But there was still the matter of the gate. We wanted the gate to be somewhere neutral so all could benefit. In the end, Ignacio was disappointed, but he accepted moving the gate, saying that if we were going to do it properly, it would not be as an individual, but as a community.

The day came when it was time to open the Women's Craft Center. BAS officials were invited to the village to witness the opening. The ladies gave them a tour of the craft center with all the gift items on display. Just then, a busload of tourists arrived at the shop to sign and see the items. The first thing they asked, "are they for sale?" People started to buy, and the women manning the gate got so amazed. I could see fire in their eyes, that this could work. For the whole day they were very active. People kept coming and going, signing the guestbook. There was a basket full of money from sales each day. That was the realization that we can work together: leadership from the women, conservationists, and community thinking.

I believe that was the hope that I had brought. It was not the only thing, but a start, to take the first steps that evolved into more ideas. I created an opportunity for them. My heart was filled with joy when they could do it for a long time. We had to do it so the wealth was distributed. They had workshops on bookkeeping and such, so they could learn to run a business.

After five years they had a celebration. They had sold $158,000 in five years! I wanted them to understand that was as a consequence of the park, if you didn't support the park, you wouldn't make this money. They could send their children to school. It was a great success!

Maya Centre Women's Group in 1999

They gave snacks, and coming to the end of the meeting, the lady giving the closing remarks thanked everyone for being with them and thanked me. Then she said they didn't need me anymore. I was sad because I would miss their company, but I was happy that they are able to do it themselves.

They always believed in me. I was always there. I wanted to prove to BAS that a group like this could work on their own. They have the opportunity to carry on this business. I didn't want it to be one of those things that gets started and then dies out.

The idea of working together was something that everyone saw was good, but you have to continue to work together. It takes awhile before you shape it. What we were doing was for everyone's well-being. As we began to progress with the idea of coming together and working toward a common goal, people understood what we were trying to do. We started to create an opportunity for ourselves. It was a great success because everybody was beginning to see that we have a lot of skills. When we put this idea together and accomplish, everybody feels good. There was a realization that this was a very good thing for a community, especially being women.

But before we became a complete success story, there were those who would want to stop it. They did not really want this to happen, or they wanted it to happen somewhere else. There was a lot of envy in the hearts of some. Envy in Maya people can become a problem. They started to bicker among themselves. There was one among them who instructed that the building should be on fire to destroy what is good. So, one night at 11:30 someone set the craft shop on fire. The community came out and fought the fire.

But this action did not stop us. Immediately we knew who it was, but because we were on this program, we all decided not to make an issue of this and move on. Let this example be a lesson for us. We know that there will be those who will not agree totally with what we are doing. It is very important that we understand each other. We decided to put aside the issue of putting the building on fire. We wanted even those people who did not agree with us to continue to follow us. One day down the road they might decide it is a good thing. This was a learning process for all of us. We were able to show what happens when you work together. And that was the only incident that happened, so I guess it was a learning for communities like us.

There are those with bright ideas who can convert the ideas into beautiful images and it flourishes, while others are not able to think quickly. Those are the ones who try to pull down the ones who are going fast. There is the need for us to talk together. If you can't paint so that it looks pretty, I can help you to make yours pretty. We have to work together. When we get to the other side, we can feel good about ourselves. We have learned. We know now that we can do things together.

Nothing like that is happening now. There are no fires. Crime is low or non-existent; drinking is not such a big deal; there are not too many drugs, just one or two people using. People still have that respect for property.

Operating on their own, the women's group did all right, but at one time we had a little problem with BAS. First they made Eugenio Ah my assistant Park Director. Then they took him to Belize City as the Protected Areas Manager.

After Eugenio Ah was named the Protected Areas Manager, the first thing he did was move the gate. I said, "Do it gradually. These people are working together and all is going well now." But he moved it just like that, suddenly it was moved.

The community burst into rage and started to block the road. The police came and said I instigated it and I was to go to jail. The conflict resolution was by Carlos Santos, who was on the BAS Board at the time. Finally BAS realized that all the other pieces need to work together. Out of that crisis came BAS' co-management project.

I had a problem with BAS at one time. It seemed they had a lack of confidence in me. The difficulties occurred with Ted Castillo when he was Executive Director. He did not believe that I was doing my work. He said he had been hearing things about me. It dragged on for a while. He wanted his program to run, but he didn't care about the communities around the Sanctuary. Community work is very delicate. You have to show that here is a way out of this problem. Let us work it together. But at that time nobody at BAS actually believed in this. It was a problem with the organization.

One day Pepe Garcia, BAS President, called and said he wanted to talk to me. He said to take the plane and he would pick me up at the airstrip. We went to his house, had something to eat, and then went out on the porch with drinks. Then he said BAS had a problem with me, that I was stealing money, buying materials for myself with the project money. He said that Christine was asking questions. Pepe told me that Christine was not sure what was happening. We are asking you to resign, and will pay you so much severance pay. I was never thinking I was going to resign.

I said to give me some direct examples; what is the evidence? I knew I had nothing to fear. I explained that my wife got money from her parents and that is how she started her business in Maya Centre.

He felt that I was pushing him around. They had already made up their minds about me. I told Pepe that I was not going to resign, not yet. Ted Castillo came to Cockscomb with Christine Anthony, the accountant, to go through the books. Ted brought me a sandwich and we walked while the accountant did her work. When we came back, she was almost finished. She said that there was no problem; the books were in order; there were no discrepancies. I said I am not surprised. Ted gave a Creole proverb, "tiger mauger, but he caca tarry," meaning that "I am so little, but I am not easy to bring down." I was clean, but I was hurt. So, I stepped down. They told me that if I had accepted the termination, I would have gotten more money, but it was not about money.

They brought Eugenio Ah to Cockscomb as Director. He improved the trail system and developed the Green Knowledge Trail. He focused on improving infrastructure, especially the sleeping areas, and added sidewalks in the Park Headquarters. When Osmany Salas became Executive Director and Valdemar Andrade was Protected Areas Manager, they came and asked me to go back. I said no at first, but then a few months later I went back.

We felt that it was good. All the parks and the communities were working together for the benefit of all. I went back as Park Director and Pedro Pixaby from Silk Grass was Assistant. After he left I began looking for someone who could take on the Director role and there came Nicacio Coc from Maya Mopan. He was willing, active, strong, had lots of ideas, and had a good grip on things. Nicacio said, "I cannot fit into your shoes," so I had to build that confidence in him. I realized he had something to offer. I could see him going to talk to the communities. I sent him to communities with difficult problems and saw him begin to lead. He explained the Sanctuary is for all of us, for the generations to come. It is all of us who will benefit. I felt he would make a good director. I wanted to be with my children. I was not around to help my older two sons with primary school, so I wanted to help with their high school and be there for the third son's primary days.

Co-management came later, but there was one flaw. They decided the village projects without talking to the communities. BAS did not have good relationships with local people. That's what often happens. The grassroots are affected most, but get the least out of these programs. If the project managers make sure to get input from the community, the people will jump on it, because they see the stepping stones. The people must be important in the process. Organizations start to fall apart because the vision is not clear. If only we are given a chance, we can try to do it. If we can't do it, then help us. That makes a "win-win" situation. People have a complete change of mind and realize our whole existence depends on the conservation of our natural resources. We are learning, tearing down, and building up new ways of thinking. A new age is coming that will do even more than we can imagine now. My oldest son, Rigoberto, is doing Natural Resource Management to make sure our environment is taken care of. I am proud of him; I am proud of the Cockscomb staff. I want an indigenous staff to prove to the world a model of management of natural resources by local, indigenous people. This model is being watched from afar.

Ernesto Saqui speaking in 1997 at the innauguration of new facilities in the Cockscomb Basin Wildlife Sanctuary.

CHAPTER 6
The Love Story

I was asked to go to Belize City to make a presentation on Cockscomb at a Protected Areas Conference about tourism and the state of the environment. They met at the Biltmore Hotel. The Conference had a section on cultural tourism, among many others. Aurora Garcia was there in that group. I never had any clue that I would look for a wife. I went to give my presentation.

That morning I started on Cockscomb, history, what we have been doing, etc. My eye caught up on a beautiful lady that stunned my interest. This person attracted me so I had to talk to her. I took a good look at her and made eye contact. When the question and answer session was finished, I walked up to the special lady and asked,"where are you from? and what are you doing?" She gave short answers and I left it like that. At the evening dinner buffet, I met her again and asked her what she was doing. She answered that she was from San Antonio Cayo, and was involved in cultural tourism, had a gift shop, and was making slate carvings with her sisters. I didn't say much. Just before the end of the conference, I asked her if she had anybody. She asked why I asked, and I said,"I want to be part of you."

She didn't want any part of it. I suggested to her if she wanted to go to her hotel that I could take her in my vehicle. She said, "No, I don't do that." It made me think it may be time for me to think about having a partner. The conference was over and I decided to try again.

I said again,"I want you to be part of my life." But in the interest of time, I asked for her contact information so I could get her to come to Maya Centre to teach the women here. She gave me her address and I wrote a few times. I was beginning to think that I wanted to be a family person. I wrote her and told her I wanted her to be my wife. She wrote back and said she thought I was married. I kept in contact and one day I visited her. Because we were discussing, she may have told her mother I was coming. Her mother met me at the gate and asked why I was there. She told me, "Go away." I said maybe just a few minutes with Aurora. I didn't have much time, so I got right to it. I told her I wanted her to be my wife. She said I think you are married and I don't want to get into the middle of family business. I said I am single and I want to marry you.

I kept writing and one day I sent her a pair of earrings, but she sent them back saying "I don't do that sort of thing." I thought,"OK maybe that is a different situation," so I did not press the issue. I was beginning to feel that it was not going to happen. I needed to figure out a way to have a better chance to talk to her. I asked the women's group if they would want to do an excursion to see how other groups do these crafts. They said that is a good idea, where? I said I know a place. The Women's Group came up with a plan to do a trip. I was so happy for this opportunity. So I wrote a letter to say that the Maya Centre Women's Group would like to do a field trip. So, they said yes we could come for a day.

I wrote her and told her I would be there and I would like to see her.

We came with everybody packed into a bus. We reached by 9 in the morning, and they were ready for us. I managed to slip away from the group and I told her I want this relationship to last forever. She said "I want this group to tell me that you don't have a wife." She asked everyone in the group if I was married and they all said no. She said "I would be interested." I asked her if she would come to my village to live. I was so happy thinking it was happening and it would change my whole life.

I kept writing, and she called me on the phone, telling me what she was doing. I said to myself, "I am an old man, I am getting older." I asked her if she would love me for who I am. She said that is not a problem, that if we are going to live together we are going to make things happen together. So now I am beginning to plan. In my culture I need to do an engagement. But she said,"my father would never let that happen."

At some point she even told me it is better I take her sister more than her. I said, "hum. When my parents send me to go shopping and they ask for sugar, I cannot get salt. I said you and no one else."

We kept going back and forth. I went back another time and told her I wanted to talk with her, but I didn't want her parents around. I asked, "If I come, would you come with me to Maya Centre?"

I needed to do some planning, because at that time I would be busy. Already I had the arrangement with Rob Horwich and Fred Coons that they would arrive at Cockscomb to plan for the black howler monkey translocation. They would arrive around the 10th of February. I wanted us to find three locations where we can build acclimatization cages and one that will be a hard release. I knew that was something I must do.

The first week of February, she said. "if you can tell me how we can get together, I will do it." I drove up there and to tell her the plan,"I will not take advantage of you or would I ever take advantage. I will be coming on Feb 14th about 9 am. That is the day we are going to live together. I don't want you to say no because I am far into this."

I didn't realize it was Valentine's Day until much later, when we were celebrating our anniversary.

The plan was that she was going to escape over wires. When she jumped the second set of wires, I would come along. I would be there at 7 pm. I told her to make sure none of her family saw her and not to bring any luggage. I talked to her at 9 in the morning to tell her the plan. I was so worried, so excited; I had butterflies.

I went to a hill to where an American guy had an eating place for tourists. He asked,"Can I help you?"

I answered,"I don't think you can help me, but I could take a cup of coffee."

He said I looked worried. "Do you know the Garcia sisters? I am preparing to get one for myself," I said.

"You mean you are going to get one? Good luck, but I doubt it," he said.

"I'm going to go and take one for myself. Like a thief in the night? Yes, that is the plan," I said. I spent practically the whole day there talking with him until the sun was going down.

"Boy oh boy I wish you good luck,"he said.

When 7 o'clock came, I saw this figure. She got in the car and we reversed as if we were going to Georgeville.

"Where are we going?" she asked. She had no idea about anybody in Georgeville, but we were not going to Georgeville. We were going to Maya Centre.

I knew this was a big change and one day I would be very happy about it. I knew it was a risky thing and not the right way to do it. But she had told me that her father would not allow it to happen the right way. She was leaving the warmth of her family to go with a stranger that she did not know.

I reassured her, "I know I am a stranger, but you can trust me and that trust will live forever with me. Whatever happens on this escape journey, I will never hurt you. I love you and I want you to be part of my life forever."

She told me, "You are a stranger, but I trust you. Don't hurt me." That was the promise we made together.

I said, "Starting today you will learn about me. Over time I will prove myself to you. Whatever happens we can work together. You can do almost the same thing that you want to do. It will not be something that is too different from what you are doing.

"For this entire journey, please trust me. Don't cry. Wherever we stop is because we are going to stop together. We are going to discuss. I will never hurt you. If anything goes wrong on this journey, we are going to be together. The important thing is that we love each other."

I could see she was developing a confidence in me. She said, "I think we can work together. We are both Maya. I think we can understand each other."

But I didn't get the sense that she was totally serious with the whole heart and mind that we could do anything we want, so it required a lot of trusting. For me that was a critical moment.

And then we kept coming down, and the night was so dark. When we looked at the road, she kept saying, "The road is empty and dark." I thought she was telling me, "I am going to the unknown."

I kept reassuring her, but I was so hurt at what I was doing because I knew this was not the right way. And I was the one causing it to happen. How much can this woman trust me? Can I be good enough to comfort her? She is a lovable person, very charismatic. Within that approach there is also that strength in her that when you come together you can feel even stronger. I could see that she was the type of person to make decisions together, but she was watching me the whole time to see how things would develop. Knowing that her parents would be looking for her, once I took her more than half of the journey, she said she was not going back. She wanted to prove to her parents that what she did was the right thing, for my sake. I would have preferred to do it the right way, but that wasn't going to happen, so we had to do what we had to do.

When she disappeared, they looked for her. Her father told one daughter to call the police because his daughter was kidnapped. But they didn't know for sure. They were looking for evidence of what had happened, but nothing was missing. She wrote a note where she was going and left it in the pillow slip so they would find it later. One sister shook the pillow slip and found it. But her mother knew.

The police set up check points. By the time we came to the junction at Roaring Creek, there was a group of security starting to establish a check point. But they hadn't set it yet, so I went through that point. I drove and drove all the way to six miles and there was a checkpoint. They had a flashlight and looked, thinking was everything OK.

"Who is this lady?"

"My Secretary, we are coming from a meeting," I answered. I drove to my parent's house, arriving after 12:30, almost 1 am. My father woke up and asked what was happening. I said this lady is going to live with me and he didn't say any more, but let us in.

The next morning I had to meet with Fred and Rob. Aurora was confused and didn't know where to go. "You are going to come with me in Cockscomb," I said. I don't think we even had breakfast.

I saw Dr. Horwich dressed up in his cap ready to go. Before I went on the trail, I asked Aurora to sit in the office with only one window open. I told her,"This is a radio and if anyone comes, push this button and tell me."

I went on the trail and Rob said we should do the Gibnut Loop first. Gibnut would be the best trail. While we walked the trail, we picked sites. I was walking about, but I wasn't with them. It was as if they were talking to a stick. We came to the first downhill and I said, "maybe this is the best place," looking at the trees and vines around.

Then I heard the radio, "they're here." I told them I brought this lady but they are after her because she didn't get permission from her father to leave.

Fred asked if I was OK, and then said, "Let's cancel this day. Is it important to you? We will help you."

We got to the Park office and the hand held radio was hanging. I wanted to check in the Dangriga police station, but I had to manage the monkey business, so I asked Rob and Fred to wait for me. But they said they would come with me. As we came down the road to Maya Centre, the road was lined with people, like the Prime Minister was here. They had seen the police going to and from Cockscomb with guns and all. I learned later that the rumor was around that I had taken this lady to Cockscomb and I was arrested.

Rob and Fred said "Let's go to the Dangriga police station."

As we were coming to the gas station at the entrance to Dangriga, I saw a pickup that looked like my wife's family vehicle heading out of town. I tried to look and see if Aurora was in the pickup, but I couldn't see.

I went to the police station. They asked me, "Who are you looking for? Do you know that what you did is illegal? I think we will arrest you."

They took me in a back room and she was sitting there. She jumped up and hugged me, saying "I have made up my mind that I want to live with you, whatever the cost, whatever the problems. This is going to be my future."

I felt so good that she realized that we had come together. We met with the understanding that we will be working together. I asked her, "Are you going to come with me, or are you going home to your parents?"

She said, "I have decided not to go with my parents, but to go with you. We are in. We are now going to live together."

I felt so good! I felt at that moment that my family life had been accomplished. I told her, "Thank you very much for putting up with all this. I am very sorry that we went through all of this, but from here on it is not going to be an easy road, but it will be manageable. We are going to journey together."

Then the community understood what happened, that I brought a woman that I did not ask permission to bring, but that she came anyway and we are going to work together.

The story was that now we are going to live happily thereafter.

My father told me I had disappointed him, "why didn't you go through the procedure? You have to take that woman back to her parents, explain why you did what you did and ask for forgiveness. You must make clear that your intention was not bad. You are going to live with this woman forever. There is no way you are going to bring this lady and you don't see her family."

A month later we went to Cayo. Her parents were cursing. They said they would accept it only if we got married. I wanted a nice Maya wedding, but they didn't give me time for that. The mother compromised, but the father didn't.

I told her father that I would feel the same, but I would make sure this finishes the right way. The father insisted that we get married. Could we do it in the next month? We got married on the 4th of April, 1992. I wanted a private ceremony in Dangriga. I talked to the priest. So he started to announce it in the bulletin. I bought the wedding dress, the ring. Her mother and siblings came, but not her father. We had a celebration at the Saqui place. Friends came. I had a plan for that day with the Golden Stream Women's Group, but when I didn't reach their meeting, they came to Maya Centre, thinking I had transportation problems, so they stayed for the wedding party.

Her family tried to get me to move to Cayo. It was difficult, never easy. But before he died, her father put a cloth on the floor and two white pillows. He made us kneel down and blessed us.

Our first son, Rigoberto, was born 15 November 1992; Juan Gabriel was born 7 March 1994; and Marroquin 23 July 2004. All were born during the day: morning, mid-morning and afternoon.

1996: Rigoberto, Aurora, Gabriel, Ernesto

26 years of Marriage

After the great marriage, we had to get to work. I continued to be the Park Director while my wife went into tourism, at first a giftshop, a campground, a restaurant, and finally turned some of the buildings into cottages. There were people coming and going to the park. It was popular for camping sites; we built guestrooms. The problem was there was no way to get to Cockscomb. She bought a small vehicle and ran a taxi. She prepared food. She started the guesthouse. She continued to take care of the children. She was able to do it all with difficulty. She was true and honest, not particular about men. She found someone who was dedicated.

Aurora was trained as a healer by her grand-uncle, Elijio Panti. After his death she continued his work and set up her clinic along with her tourism business at our home in Maya Centre.

Going through primary education in Maya Centre, secondary at Ecumenical, and 6th form Junior College, our older two sons were successful at both the high school and Junior College level.

Rigoberto graduated from the University of Belize with a Bachelors degree in Natural Resource Management. He did a project in Hopkins on climate change and garbage. At the end of five weeks, they did a report. He was selected to present at the research symposium at UB and again in the U.S. He is working in Pantera's jaguar research. He is following in his father's footsteps. He is looking at our environment and asking, "how can we make it better?"

Juan Gabriel attended St. Jude R. C. Primary School and Stann Creek Ecumenical High School. He graduated from Stann Creek Ecumenical College with an Associate Degree. Presently he works with us, his parents, in our tourism business and is working hard to reopen business. We have been able to provide the children the opportunity to go to school and to see the next thing. They see the business we do; they can continue this business or do their own thing.

Marroquin is the baby. He seems to be following his mother. Maybe he will be an herbalist. He gets the herbs for her and is actually there to see what his mother is doing. He likes nature. He is interested in rocks. There is something a little different from the other two. He tries to explain the little he knows. The other part of him, he is trying to get into cooking, looking at cooking shows on TV. He saw corndogs and made them. He will say to his mother, "I feel a little bad. I want you to do a little healing." He is independent; he has a bit of comfort, a very easy going guy.

Juan Gabriel Saqui and Cladia Carlota Nunez have been living together for about six years in Maya Center Village. Cladia Carlota Nunez is from the beautiful village of Hopkins. She attended Holy Family Primary School after which she persued her high school education at Stann Creek Ecuemenical High School. They have two very healthy children, a boy, Ernesto Luke Saqui, and a beautiful daughter Azlynn Aurora Carlota Saqui. Ernesto attends St. Jude Roman Catholic Primary School and is already a promising young computer wizard. As parents we love them both and their children.

I am happy for my accomplishments. But most of all I am grateful for sharing my experiences as a Maya and the culture that I hope will continue to survive.

(*back row, from left*) Rigoberto, holding Azlynn Aurora Carlota, Marroquin, Gabriel, Cladia; (*sitting, from left*) Ernesto, holding Ernesto Luke, Aurora

CHAPTER 7
Illness

Cultural ceremony is part of daily life for Maya people. If you don't do it regularly, there can be a spell or bad experiences. One can get sick. I had the experience of being sick. I got so sick to the point of not knowing what is happening to me. I became weak and thin; I was no longer eating. It was not me. My eyes would not focus, so my vision was fuzzy like I am looking through a screen. Every time I went to sleep, I could feel myself dropping down as if in a drum. I could see this white road in the night and it made me want to run away. I was so worried, so sick and thin, that I had to also stop my work in Cockscomb.

My wife said I should go to the doctor. He examined me, and found nothing wrong. He gave me pills that I was to take it in the event that something feels wrong, but they were of no help.

After we had exhausted what the doctor could provide, I went to a healer in Maya Mopan. He looked at me, examined me, and did the traditional pulse healing. "Oh my!" he said, "you are going to be crazy. You are meant to run around like crazy and keep going." I never thought anything could be so wrong.

He gave me some herbal medicine that I was to grind and take as a bath the next day at exactly six o'clock. So I ground it and I put one calabash full over my head. But it was like someone hit me over the head with a mallet; I almost screamed. So I stopped the medicine but then I got worried even more. I don't know where I am going to go because the doctor couldn't help and this medicine won't work. Should I go back to the healer?

My wife then said she believed she could help me and I said I was open to that. She prepared her medicine. Just walking from the house to the restaurant I was so weak that I had to lie down in a hammock. She gave me the medicine. I think it was skunk root. The medicine tasted so bad that I wanted to throw up, but I drank the whole glass. I sat back in the hammock and dropped asleep. That happened about 9 am and I slept until 1:30 pm. As I woke up, I noticed a big difference in myself. I felt light; my eyes were not blurred; I didn't feel weak, that made me feel that I would get better.

I was so hungry, which I hadn't been for a long time. My wife prepared a soup. I started to take the soup, cleaned the whole dish, ate like a crazy person. I felt filled up, the day looked so good. I saw a new me. My wife gave me another cup of this medicine, I wanted to throw up again. I went to sleep, but when I woke up later, I felt like I was back to normal. I began to feel different. I slept and got up the next morning, and it was even better. After a week I got up, and in a week and a half, my body started building up. In four weeks I was like a normal person. Up to this point I don't know what happened to me. I had a bad feeling and felt like giving up, but I got this medicine and I am a normal person again.

There are times in our life that we must understand that there are negative forces and positive forces that can make you or break you. This was a negative experience. We tend to forget the natural world and forget to give thanks. This is calling for an activity to give thanks to God, or the owner of whatever we were promised and are using. Maya people realize that we have to give thanks, to make ceremonies, especially if we have things in our lives that we use every day, things where gods own the elements. We can be greedy and never want to pay back and that is when we get into trouble.

CHAPTER 8
Politics

I wanted to get into politics to do the right thing for the people, but I didn't know that you have to be corrupted. In 2002 Henry Canton resigned and didn't complete his five-year term, which began when he was elected in 1998. Somebody had to be the new standard-bearer and then run in 2003, so I decided to challenge the position. I started campaigning in 2002. I wanted to be an Area Representative. I know the local problems. I know the cry of our people, so I decided I was going to offer myself. But Dr. Canton supported Rodwell Ferguson. I went head-on into the campaign, thinking I was doing very well. I didn't realize that there are people who must make things go their way. That is what happened. There were three of us, Rodwell, me, and Gasper Martinez from Hopkins. Because it was likely that I would win, all of a sudden, Dr. Elizabeth Zabaneh decided to run, so she took some of the votes that would have come to me. The convention was in Silk Grass. They were going to close it at 4 pm, but then they decided to hold it open until 6 and that is where it went wrong. People from Placencia came and Rodwell Ferguson came in first, I came in second, then Elizabeth, and then Martinez from Hopkins. That was the way the election went. I realized it was never going to happen for me.

It was a short and difficult campaign, a lesson learned for me. There were people who were really disappointed when I lost. I decided I was going to step back and leave politics altogether. But that is not easy to do.

Before the 2003 national election, Rodwell Ferguson told me, "We have to win this election. It is not about me." He was always worried about my involvement. He would feed me information, but had never asked me to be on any committees.

After the 2003 election, the entire village of Maya Centre had an uprising. The village wrote a petition listing things that I was not doing. I was called a thief, saying I stole money; that I was suppressing people; that I was doing all for myself and not the village. Everybody came against me, even Hermelindo, my brother. There was a lot of chaos and word was that I would be kicked out by this government that I supported.

I thought Rodwell was behind that uprising, so I went to Belmopan and had a meeting with Rodwell. He said to me, "You had better step down. As the Minister, I should listen to our people. I am asking you to step down."

I said, "This is constitutional. The people voted me in. Until there is evidence that I stole, I should remain as Village Council Chair."

I went to see the CEO in Local Government, E. Roy Cayetano. I told him what was happening and said I needed his help. I explained that I was getting no help from the Area Representative to fix the roads or do anything in the village. He said that is not your responsibility, but it is Rodwell's problem.

I asked for an audience with the Prime Minister, the CEO, two other people from the Ministry, and Rodwell. The Prime Minister said, "I am going to tell you in this office, all of us are from the same house. Why is it that we want one of us to leave? Rodwell, this man, the Chair of Maya Centre, must stay. I asked Lillian Zyden to look through all the records and she signed a report that nothing was wrong. Rodwell, these roads not fixed, but that is your responsibility. You are making it difficult. This man was elected by the people. We will leave it until the time is right. We can't tell him to go."

Roy organized a village meeting the next month, making sure all the people who were organizing the protest came. Everybody thought the meeting was to get me to step down. The Liberator newspaper was invited.

Time came for the meeting. Roy explained that it is not easy to ask a leader to step down. That is not how it works. There was big booing. He said there has to be proof that the leader was stealing or is insane. He asked Lillian Zayden, the accountant, to report on her findings when she checked the books. She said that everything was in order. There were no discrepancies.

Roy continued by asking, what are the problems? The roads need fixing; village projects are not done. Who should do it? He told them that the Area Representative had the responsibility to fix the roads and give the Village Council the resources to do the village projects, but he is not cooperating. We can't change this person. It wouldn't hold in court because he is still doing what he is supposed to do. We need to work together.

The reporter from the *Liberator* kept asking questions. He wrote about community issues; how we have to work together. Without support from the government, the Village Council doesn't have resources to do these things.

Rodwell said, "The Chair is clean. It would be unconstitutional to remove him when he has done no wrong. There is no one to blame. All of us work as a team."

Then everything began to die down. Some understood; some just left. I realized that when people want to make an issue of something they can, whether there is any truth to it. But when you do your work legally, there is nothing they can do. Rodwell came to see me. I was in my hammock and he came and said, "I am very sorry."

I told him, "You are forgiven because now you have to fix things in Maya Centre and the roads."

After that chaotic moment, when the next Village Council election came, I did not allow myself to be put down. I ran again and won. I do these things, not because I want the power, but because I

(*from left*) Rodwell Ferguson, Aurora Saqui, Prime Minister Said Musa, Ernesto Saqui

know there are things that must be set in place. We are a deprived people; we have to look after our needs: land, infrastructure, electricity, extra land for growth of the village. We hired private teachers to help with the school, encouraged kindergarten. I don't have a baby, so this is not for my family. This is the hope for the community. We need to think ahead and look after little ones, to send the children to school. That is the reality today, the way forward. We have to stay on course, and it takes leaders to make it happen. That's the way we are going to reach to the next level. We are Maya people, but we can go to University. It doesn't mean that you lose your language, your culture, your food. All that is special, so don't try to be who you aren't. In the days when I was in the Village Council, I said these things. This is what drives me to be a leader.

I find dealing with people very hard. I have never disrespected people. I don't go out of bounds and call names. I say, "let's move in this direction, there shouldn't be any enemies." But politics divided us. The more churches we had, the more hatred showed itself.

I decided in 2010 that it was enough and encouraged other people to run. They ran and they won. I am less involved in the Village Council now. I have done my part. We have enough young people who can look at what we want for our community.

Bobby Leslie and Wil Maheia wanted me to join them after I was not in the Village Council any more. They came and asked me to join them, saying they would merge the VIP with the PNP. But I decided I am not ready, and the country is not ready for a third party.

I know the issues. My wife is telling me, "You have encouraged them. You should take it slower now. Best you come and work on our business." So I am not really active now.

After all these problems, them saying I am terrible, I am this, I am that, they wanted to build a monument in front of the school with four palms in my honour. I accepted it because it is my people saying that they know I have done some good. They dedicated it on my birthday, November 7th, 2009. They were going to do a celebration every November 7th, but I said that is asking too much.

The award reads: *Dedicated to Ernesto Saqui for 26 years of outstanding contribution and achievement for Maya Centre Village as Village Council Chairman from 1984-2010 November 9th, 2009.*

They picked that day to celebrate all that work. After 26 years from the actual beginning of the village, much has been done to develop the village. Any activity that is development for the people to have a better way of life, we did it: From the women's craft center, the school, social services, health center, water, electricity, telephone, soliciting computers for the school. We exploited the opportunities  that tourism brought. We developed Bed and Breakfast lodging, tour-guiding, all as a consequence of the relationship with Cockscomb. A high percentage of our young people are going to high school as a mandatory step to higher education. There is open support for all school programs in this village. A lot of our students who got education come back as teachers, working in tourism, or hospitality. It is all about development, making life better. In the end, people who take advantage derive a benefit.

Ernesto Saqui with Nieces and Nephews:
(from *left standing*) Javier Saqui, Regina Saqui, Anita Saqui, Luis Navarro
(*from left sitting*) Rudy Saqui, Ernesto Saqui, Violeta Saqui
Photo courtesy Pio Saqui

Winter Solstice Ceremony 2014 at Nim Li Punit Maya Site
Aurora (*center*) and Ernesto Saqui (*right*)

CHAPTER 9
Knowing Who We Are

Who Will Grow the Food?

The old people say when you see birds boring your corn, there will be hunger. When there is not enough for the birds to eat in their world, they come to eat. Now animals are attacking our plantations. It used to be that you might lose only a little, but now we are losing a lot. It is a sign of the times. We will be having less. Where does that put the Maya man? Those who are not going to school.

Somebody has to grow the food. In school, there used to be a program where students learned to grow food, but that program got stopped. Young people these days prefer to go to work. You will never get rich growing food. It is a challenge for this Maya culture. They look down on agriculture. Nobody wants to dirty their clothes. We are at a crossroad. We have to figure it out. In Maya Centre there are only about 20 per cent making farms and they are over 50 years old. Nobody is growing rice, only corn and a little beans. If farming had a financial benefit, everyone would do it. But everyone is going to school to find jobs and don't want to do farming. It takes time to do it and sometimes you are not successful. We are giving up. We are lazy to do agriculture.

We must never lose sight of who we are.

If I have the mindset, I will be comfortable and feel good about myself. I want the younger people to understand that there is nothing wrong with being educated, to live a comfortable life. Except that you must know who you are as a person. Once you know who you are, you are comfortable among other people. We feel nervous and afraid to say the wrong things and be put down for that. We are never really encouraged to speak our mind freely. We are always limiting ourselves. It is really for the young people to understand that being part of a Maya group does not subtract anything from us. We have to keep practicing and sharing our culture. We shouldn't be concerned. Garifuna people always talk in their own language; but Maya are shy to talk in their own language in front of others. We want to encourage young people to feel good about themselves and speak out. Don't be ashamed about your culture and do what you have to do.

Now things are changing. An older man planted his beans two years ago. The beans came up but the rains didn't come. And then when they did come, there was flooding. It is climate change. Now we have to chance the weather, and plant anyway. Ideally what we are talking about is maintaining the consistency. Some people are losing faith. They think it is better to go buy in the market. A lot of us will stop doing farming. It is easier to get educated and get a job. Then you have money to go buy food. That is easier than growing your own food.

Compadre-Comadre Relationships

The status of a family in a Maya community sometimes plays an important role. Community members take advantage of community individuals who have a good standing with great self-respect, good family practices, who are from God-fearing and law-abiding families, people who live exemplary lives. It is this kind of families that are sought to become god-parents. Parents who want to have their children baptized, get confirmed or married look for such people to become witnesses for their children for baptism, confirmation or marriages. Those are some of the traits sought if the children are to be raised in the right direction. It takes both parents and god-parents to help children grow into adults who will have good families. Becoming godparents is the prize for being an outstanding family in any community, but it is also a serious responsibility.

You also become the comadre or compadre for life for the parents of those who get baptized, confirmed or married. The candidates that get baptized confirmed, married will always call the witnesses "godmother" and "godfather". This established respect will be for life. If this respect is ever broken, then either the godchildren deliberately intended to make it this way in order not to continue to live the life of respect. Or they have fallen short of that understanding so that there must be another round of counseling to re-establish the respect that must be followed at all times. The occasion of baptism or confirmation or marriage is taken as a serious moment. There is usually a great celebration at the family's residence with food and drinks. Sometimes there is also a lot of adult drinking in honor of the occasion. Many times the feasting has a great ending.

You will know when the opportunity presents itself. Usually, you get a surprise home visit by the persons who need their sons or daughters to be baptized, confirmed or married. Fortunately, I have been a compadre twelve times for baptism and confirmation, and a witness for over a dozen marriages.

Juuntulico'on

I wanted to develop a new organization, Juuntulico'on, because I felt that whatever I have done in leadership of the community is already becoming a reality because the community has benefited and is developing as I was hoping it would. The shaping of the community has already been taken care of. Now it is time to move on to another aspect of the Maya dream.

We have forgotten about being Maya. We were very careful of the whole story made of 2012 as if it were the end of the world, but that was not what the Maya people predicted. We cannot let ourselves accept that kind of notion. We have to create something, so how can we develop a new program? The Maya community has been moving as a Maya community and will be here for a long time. We have nowhere else to go. Along with the 2012 activities coming to an end we said, "Let us organize ourselves." How can we do that? We can do activities that can show what we do as Maya people, parts of us, the Maya people, that have never been highlighted.

We have to unite. We have to ensure that all Maya people come together and work toward one goal. So we developed an organization, Juuntulioco'on, which means "one Maya people." Another side of it means "together we move forward."

We wanted to move forward together. It is not necessary to destroy the 2012 story, but to sustain our heritage practice of who we are as Maya people: food, language, clothing, lifestyle, all things that speak of Maya culture. One way we can bring it forward is for me to make it work for our people. I thought it would be good: no politics, religion, or community problems, just talking about bringing our Maya identity forward, seeking recognition in the way we do our life as Maya people. Even though we might be in different villages, towns, and countries, we are still Maya people and we can still work together.

We wanted to register the organization so we would have recognition as we can speak with one voice. So we registered Juuntulico'on. Now we can work on what is the goal of the organization, promoting Maya culture through research, programming and advocacy.

What is our history? What are the basic needs? We felt this could include cultural preservation, making sure that we have programs that will be for the purpose of education. When we do that we are preserving our culture.

It will help to unite us so we can work together as we promote the Maya culture. Maya people feel deprived or have a low self-esteem. They always feel there are people better than us. We want to develop pride in ourselves and awareness of the Maya way of life in others. We can celebrate contributions by Maya people.

Culturally there are things that we do. But because it is cultural, the rest of the country doesn't care, thinking, that is just the Maya culture. We want recognition. We want to be known for what and who we are. Maya people have always been ashamed. They were afraid to bring people into their home because it has a thatched roof. But that is the way we live and we want recognition. There are many who would like to express themselves, but they don't speak English, so we want to be the voice of the voiceless.

Politicians always say the Mayans don't need water because they can wash in the river. They don't have need electricity for anything that they do. But just because we wash in the stream doesn't mean that we don't need clean fresh water like everyone else or that I don't have use for the conveniences of electricity. It is an issue of the unbalancing of service distribution.

Yes I am a cultural person, but that doesn't mean that I should be denied conveniences of modern life. Living culturally, keeping our traditions is not living in the past. It doesn't mean that I don't want to move forward. This is the way I tell my story. I shouldn't be prevented from using the conveniences of life.

Some of the first activities of Juutulico'on were familiarization meetings where we talk to our people about not getting what we need and let others know what we are doing.

Maya Ceremony, May 11, 2019 (*above*) San Roman, Stann Creek District, (*below*) San Antonio, Cayo District, Belize

We are collecting legends, seeking sources where we can get these lessons, wherever we can find them. The monkey and the jaguar, for example, is a Maya legend.

Our Maya ceremonies and spirituality recognize that Mother Earth gives us strength. We live off the strength of the forest where we get medicine, food, and materials for shelter. In Maya ceremonies we seek attention to receive from the forests for needs that help us in our lifetime. I make my intention in the forest. I may ask for success. The forest gives me wisdom. We have to provide the space for all these animals in the forest.

Maya ceremonies are important, like initiations for young boys. But keeping these Maya traditions doesn't subtract anything from the rest of life. We can go to university, have a profession, and still practice our Maya culture.

We are learning about Maya hieroglyphic phonetic translation. Recent science has uncovered the phonetic meaning of various images in the glyphs on stelae found in ancient Mayan sites. The stelae tell stories about life that was lived at that time. We can now go back and translate. We have had three or four workshops with the epigraphers who know the phonetic meanings of images on the glyphs. They can pronounce these, but don't know what it means. We hear them and understand the words in our Mayan language. These workshops are very important opportunities for the participants. There were 29 participants on Jan 7, 2018, who can now write their name in glyphs. Those doing the slate carving now know what the glyph means. It is good for carvers, for students, and for those who buy the carvings who now know the meaning.

We are looking at the past and bringing it to the forefront. We can live with pride for how we live, what we know, and what we can talk about. That provides the opportunity to teach about our Mayan ways. We have been given the opportunity to conduct Maya ceremonies at the ancient sites. Here is where we survived.

Principally those are the three main ideas of Juuntulico'on: 1) Research on Maya culture, history and needs, including educational programming and cultural preservation. 2) Maya cultural pride and awareness, including cultural programs and contributions by Mayans. 3) Unity of Maya people in and beyond Belize, including serving as a voice for the voiceless and networking beyond our borders. Let every step we take be a step toward Maya cultural pride and unity!

Ernesto Saqui, 2019